TOM LOWRY

LEADER IN A THOUSAND

TOM LOWRY

LEADER IN A THOUSAND

Bill Francis

TRIO
BOOKS

FRONT COVER:
Peter McIntyre's painting of "The Grove" at Okawa.

National Library of New Zealand Cataloguing-in-Publication Data

Francis, Bill, 1947-
Tom Lowry : leader in a thousand / Bill Francis.
Includes bibliographical references and index.
ISBN 978-0-9582839-8-4
1. Lowry, Tom, 1898-1976. 2. Cricket players—New Zealand
—Biography.
I. Title.
796.358092—dc 22

Published in 2010 by Trio Books Ltd, PO Box 17021, Wellington.
www.triobooks.co.nz

Book design, including front and back covers, by Sally McIntosh.
Printed by Astra Print, Wellington.

Contents

Introduction

In a passing parade of New Zealand cricket legends, some written about, some sadly forgotten, Tom Lowry stands out as one of the most pivotal figures. He, as much as anyone, laid the foundations for the development and acceptance of New Zealand cricket on the international stage. He captained our first two teams to England and managed the third. He led New Zealand in their first official test. He captained Cambridge University and played county cricket for Somerset. While at Cambridge, he was selected in Archie MacLaren's MCC team that toured New Zealand and Australia. His extraordinary, unmatched playing and captaincy record was just one aspect of Tom's life in cricket.

When Tom died, Dick Brittenden, New Zealand's best cricket writer, described him as probably the most colourful character in the whole history of New Zealand cricket. Nothing much has changed in the last 30-odd years to alter that view, and so the verdict can stand.

Because of his immense strength and size, and the colour of his on-field and off-field commentary, he drew comparisons with England's WG Grace and Australia's Warwick Armstrong, two big men and larger-than-life cricket legends. The comparisons were justified, but as in the cases of WG and "The Big Ship" (Armstrong), some stories about Tom are exaggerated, some apocryphal. Sorting out the real from the fictitious has been a challenge, but all of those related in this story clearly reflect Tom the person, and his attitude to the game and its players.

These facts were just a starting point in contemplating a biography on Tom. There was much more. His two sisters married his close friends. One of them, Percy Chapman, became captain of England cricket at the same time Tom was captaining New Zealand, while the other, Reg Bettington, was captain of Oxford (when Tom captained Cambridge), later captained New South Wales, played for an Australian X1 and became the Australian amateur golf champion. The Lowry sisters who married Chapman and Bettington, Beet and Marion, were characters in their own right. These marriages produced a beguiling and unique family sports triumvirate.

And then, underlying this cricket background was the fascinating heritage of the Lowry family. They were pioneer Hawke's Bay settlers and developed a property, Okawa, that was not only a sheep station of significant proportions and productivity, but eventually became home to a horse stud that bred and raced some of New Zealand's best.

Tom, taking a running leap from cricket into racing, became as prominent in that world as he had in cricket.

The family, by its own endeavours and aided by some marriage partnerships (particularly between Tom's father and mother), was at times wealthy beyond belief. Because of this, Tom occasionally had to contend with the modern-day tall poppy syndrome. But even though he was probably New Zealand's richest cricketer ever, no-one ever carried it with less fanfare, less ostentation. This ever-widening canvas became a compelling motivating factor in wanting to put Tom's life in print.

Once set upon the journey, the help of the Lowry family has been unfailingly positive. Tom's three surviving children have been a pleasure to get to know and to talk to about their father. Tom Junior and Joanna at Okawa and Pat and Jane in Taupo have welcomed me and my wife, Mary, into their homes during the researching of this book, while Carol, from her base in Christchurch, has kept up a rapid-fire email response to my many pleas for details and clarification.

Staying at Okawa on two occasions was like being in Tom's presence, so overpowering was the strength and history of Tom and the family. The famous photos hang in the halls, the stud books line the library, the homestead, gardens and paddocks could have stood still for 100 years. From Tom Junior, Pat and Carol, one got a strong sense of the welcoming, openness and kindness that Tom displayed throughout his life.

Other wider family members, notably Ralph Lowry's sons, Peter and Robin, were also most helpful. In England, Vicky Thomas, Reg and Marion Bettington's only child, assisted enormously to enable the chapter on Reg Bettington to be written.

Many others happily agreed to interviews or supplied information, background and support. They included: Jane Teal, the Christ's College's archivist, who went beyond the call of duty providing me details of Tom's Christ's College days; Ray Saunders (and his complete run of *Wisdens*); Jim Allnat; Bryan Haggitt; Peg Vivian; Ian Mackersey (with aviation advice); Iain Gallaway; Peter Sellers; Jim Newbegin; Scott Francis; Mike Batty; Ron Palenski of the New Zealand Sports Hall of Fame; Warwick Larkins; Haddon Donald; Pamela Fowler; Elaine Wheeler; Graham Potter (bearing photographs from Maadi); Don Neely; Alex Hedley; Eddie Lowry; Steve Brew; Rob Franks; Barry Gustafson; Alan Richards and Sir Patrick Hogan, who fondly recalled his first visit to Okawa. My broadcasting PA, Anne-Marie Gibson, deserves a medal for her patience and expertise in handling a wide variety of tasks. Above all, Mary, my wife, encouraged, advised and supported, and was a special touchstone for farming and horse matters.

An extensive range of written sources were used and special mention should be made of some. Henry Esmond Blair Newton, known to all as "Newt", a one-time cricket historian, compiled a number of stories from the Okawa cricket days on the Grove and a variety of these have been used in chapter 11. David Kynaston wrote comprehensively on Archie MacLaren's MCC tour in 1922-23, Mike Batty's work on the 1927 tour and Budge Hintz's 1931 tour book were most valuable. Others, including Dick Brittenden, Mathew Appleby, Nigel Smith, Lynn McConnell and Don Neely, had written interesting profiles that helped immeasurably. In addition, I couldn't have done without the scrapbooks of the 1931 and 1937 tours loaned to me by Graham Vivian. They were compiled by his grandfather for his son Giff (Graham's father).

Graham also provided photos from the 1931 tour, but the bulk of the photographs for the book have been supplied from the Lowry family collections (Tom Junior, Pat and Carol); Vicky Thomas (on Reg Bettington); and from the impressive collections of Don Neely and Joseph Romanos. Others came from my own collection, and from Graham Potter, Ron

Palenski and Rob Franks.

Tom's old team-mate, Raymond Robertson-Glasgow, in his superb writing on the game, among other complimentary remarks, once described Tom thus: "He was a remarkable cricketer, strong versatile, courageous, original and a leader in a thousand. He was a man first and a cricketer second, but it was a close finish." This telling description of leadership in cricket eventually extended way beyond the scope of the summer game – thus the fitting sub-title to this book.

It was Joseph Romanos, a long-time friend, who encouraged me to get writing on Tom Lowry and through his editorial and publishing skills with Trio Books enabled the project to come to fruition. Joseph was certain it would be an enjoyable experience and he was right. And then, to cap it off, Sir Ron Brierley, a wonderful friend of cricket, gave financial backing to enable the book to proceed, as he has done with several other New Zealand cricket biographies.

The Lowry tradition of naming the oldest son of each generation Tom has not made for ease of understanding as to which Tom is which. For the purposes of this story, the settler at Okawa is always Thomas. His son is always referred to as TH and his son, the subject of this biography, is always referred to as Tom. His son is Tom Junior. Tom Junior also has a son, known as Tommy, the current lease-holder of Okawa.

For reference, they are, in order of generation:

Thomas

TH

Tom

Tom Junior

Tommy

I've lived with Tom Lowry for the past year. I lay on the grass on the boundary and visualised him taking an attack apart, eavesdropped on his running commentaries, wandered out and, against the backdrop of the towering poplars, inspected the Grove concrete pitch and its covering, sampled his many kindnesses at the Okawa dining table, slept in one of the upstairs bedrooms alongside the trunk of memories, looked out the window at the mares and foals grazing in a distant paddock. He may not have been there physically, but he was very real to me.

BILL FRANCIS

Auckland

January 2010

1. Punching Above Our Weight

"Sensation at Lord's", "MCC team routed", "Zealots of New Zealand", "Lowry Inspiring" – all snatches of headlines decorating the daily newspapers, both home and abroad, one exceptional day in 1931. While they signalled a triumphant cricket victory for New Zealand, the impact of that day went far beyond another tick in the plus column of a tour record. This was an achievement against the inventors and rulers of the great game; indeed, at their own headquarters, where many actually played the game for a living and, furthermore, it was recorded by a team of "weekend players" of little repute, the self-confessed minnows of the game.

"Punching above our weight" is a metaphor now so ingrained in the New Zealand lexicon that it has become accepted as a truism, beyond argument. Trotted out with a clichéd precision by politicians (but enhanced by the heroism of our servicemen and women in major conflicts), it covers our stand against nuclear ships (the mouse that roared), can extend as far back as the ground-breaking legislation of women's suffrage and social security, and can telescope forward to the 1980s free-market economic policies.

We like its use because it overcomes an inferiority complex based on our diminutiveness, our remoteness and sometimes the snideness by Australians, in particular, to sheep far out-numbering the population. We claim, with justifiable pride, the successes and achievements of Ernest Rutherford, Kiri Te Kanawa, Ed Hillary, Professor William Liley, Katherine Mansfield and Peter Jackson et al.

But "punching above our weight" belongs best where it originated – among the endeavours of sports heroes, a place where it's expressed with meaning and passion. Go back over a century to the visit of a Great Britain rugby side, beaten by New Zealand in a result hailed the length and breadth of the country. Then just a year later, in 1905, when a team, now known as the New Zealand "All Blacks", demolished the might of the United Kingdom with the exception of Wales (after the disallowing of a try that many people believed had been scored by a player named Deans).

The rugby surge continued with the Invincibles' tour of the United Kingdom in 1924-25, when players such as Nepia, Cooke and Brownlie became not only New Zealand heroes, but

George Nepia was one of the stars of the Invincibles rugby team that so captured the attention of British sports fans.

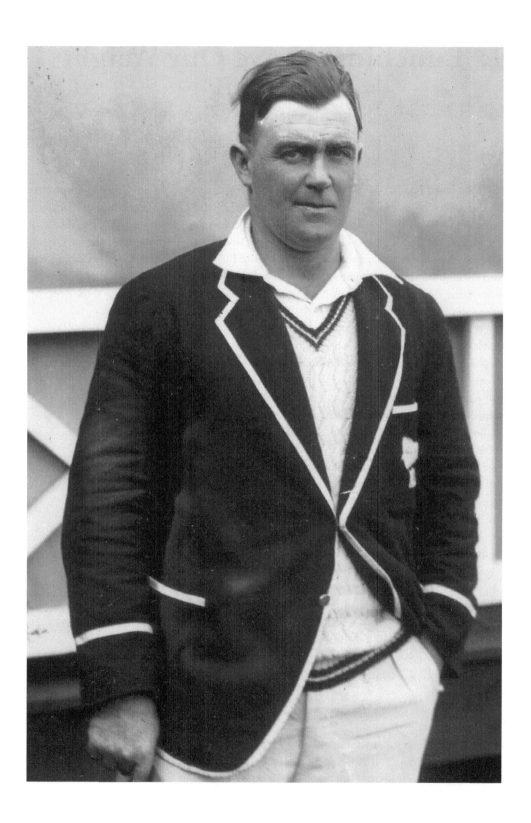

excited an "away" viewing audience as well.

It wasn't only rugby that was proving a good "puncher" on the world stage: Anthony Wilding, from a wealthy Christchurch cricket family, became four times Wimbledon singles tennis champion: Billy Webb, Dick Arnst and Darcy Hadfield all became world single sculls rowing champions in the early years of the 20th century; Arthur Porritt picked up a sprint bronze at the 1924 Paris Olympics; Ted Morgan won a boxing gold medal at the 1928 Amsterdam Olympics; and in the same year "The Hard Rock from Down Under", Tom Heeney, fought Gene Tunney for the world heavyweight boxing title at Yankee Stadium in New York in front of 46,000 spectators.

If there was one notable sports exception to this early propensity to become attention-grabbers on wider fields it was, surprisingly, cricket, which was played in New Zealand as early as the 1840s. After a visit by George Parr's English team in 1863-64, international cricket in New Zealand became ever more frequent, and by the 1890s there were quite regular international exchanges.

These early tours generally featured Australian state sides. A full Australian test X1 didn't consistently play New Zealand until 1973-74 (there had been one official test against Australia in 1946). Otherwise New Zealand generally had to make do with playing touring combinations from England or full MCC sides that tacked on a few matches in New Zealand after a full-scale Ashes series in Australia.

Casting a critical eye back over New Zealand's chequered cricket history, its stunted growth owes much to the sheer disdain displayed by its closest neighbour, Australia, a cricket powerhouse that, with an ounce of benevolence and an eye to the global future of the game, could have, at a much earlier time, stopped walking round with its nose in the air at the mere mention of cricket in the "Shaky Isles".

The statistics are revealing. By the time New Zealand played their second official test against Australia, in 1973-74, they had met England 43 times in tests, South Africa 17, India 16, Pakistan 15 and West Indies 14. Of course, there were other reasons for New Zealand's lack of advancement, including lack of finance, a paucity of coaches, inadequate pitches and inept umpiring. But Australia cricket's snobbishness still rankles and is not easily forgotten.

Fortunately, much less of a sniffy attitude emanated from the home of cricket, and it was to the MCC that New Zealand frequently turned. Pelham Warner, captaining Lord Hawke's team to New Zealand in 1903, regarded our best XI as superior to the best of the second-class English counties and equal to the last of the first-class counties. Three years later, Teddy Wynyard, in charge of another touring English team, believed the game in New Zealand had scarcely advanced beyond infancy. While these were variable verdicts, the game still had an enthusiastic following. It was (and still is) the national summer sport, but there was much to be done to make any significant progress on the world cricket stage.

While the Warner and Wynyard-led teams pinpointed weaknesses and probably did more than anything to encourage the importing of professional coaches, other factors caused the progress to be so pedestrian. War was one. Before World War I and then in its aftermath, there were occasional exchanges across the Tasman, New Zealand playing state sides when

LEFT: Tom, ready for action. A "leader in a thousand" – strong, confident, in charge.

9

touring and the Australians generally sending sub-strength combinations to play unofficial tests and meet the major associations and some provincial teams. There was a span of 16 years between Wynyard's 1906-07 English team and the next MCC visit, by Archie McLaren's team, in 1922-23.

The game was advancing slower than a Geoff Boycott century. But then after much planning and consultation, New Zealand, in 1927, made its first tour to England, followed four years later by another, but this time with enhanced status and acceptance as an emerging cricket country worthy of consideration and recognition.

The captain of the 1931 New Zealand team wasn't your archetypal cricketer. Built more like a ranging middle-row forward, at over 6ft and close to 14st, Tom Lowry had a powerhouse body capable of chucking around a 175kg wool bale. He had hands to match, capable of clubbing a ball many a mile and equally ready to snaffle a catch in the field or behind the stumps.

When the hands weren't in use on the field, the fingers invariably carried a burning cigarette. You could see the cricketer was a man of the land. The determined blue-grey eyes were practised at casting a penetrating glance over stock, but just as equally across a cricket field and particularly opposing batsmen. The strong handsome face had weathered a bit, exposed to the countryside farming elements, as well as from endless summer days on the cricket field. The hair was thick and brushed down, now often protected by a familiar Homburg, and not only recreationally. Lowry had no compunction about wearing it on to the field if that's what the conditions demanded.

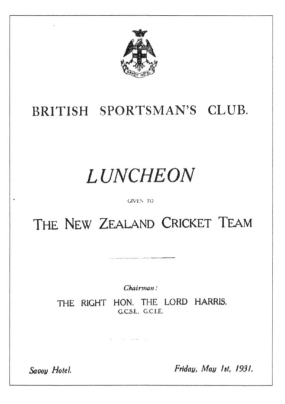

BRITISH SPORTSMAN'S CLUB.

LUNCHEON

GIVEN TO

THE NEW ZEALAND CRICKET TEAM

Chairman:
THE RIGHT HON. THE LORD HARRIS.
G.C.S.I., G.C.I.E.

Savoy Hotel. *Friday, May 1st, 1931.*

When Lowry took his team to Lord's for the MCC match in 1931, the fourth "test" of the tour, the side had already cleaned out a powerful Essex team by an innings in their opening match, with Dempster getting a double-hundred and Merritt an eight-wicket haul. They had played well in commanding draws against Leicestershire and Hampshire, highlighted by a further century to Dempster and one to Page, and Cromb had snaffled a five-wicket bag. Now they were ready to be measured by the English cricket establishment, as well as the public, as to their prospects for the forthcoming test (only one was planned at that stage) and the wider tour.

TABLE A.

Lord Harris
T. C. Lowry
Lord Desborough
Field-Marshal Viscount Plumer and Guest
Sir Archibald Weigall
Lord Leigh
Lord Ebbisham
Sir Kynaston Studd
Sir Thomas Wilford
Earl Jellicoe
M. L. Page
Earl Howe

TABLE B.

Lord Decies
  Guest, Sir James O'Grady
  Guest, Major Larcombe
  Guest, Duncan McClure
  Guest, Hon. George Beresford
C. F. W. Allcott
R. C. Blunt
Sir F. W. Lewis
  Guest, C. J. Cowan
Colonel Phillips
  Guest, General Wigan
Sir Edwin K. Stockton

TABLE C.

Admiral Sir Hugh Watson
I. B. Cromb
Lt.-Col. Sir Henry Galway
H. D. Swan
Sir Charles Allom
  Guest,
Col. Laurence Carr
T. H. Carlton Levick
Major J. B. Paget
Admiral C. S. Hickley
C. S. Dempster
A. H. H. Gilligan

TABLE D.

Noel Curtis-Bennett
  Guest, Sir Malcolm Campbell
J. L. Kerr
A. P. F. Chapman
  Guest,
  Guest,
  Guest,
  Guest,
  Guest,
K. C. James
M. J. C. Allom
K. S. Duleepsinhji
G. B. Legge
E. T. Benson
E. W. Dawson
W. Findlay

TABLE E.

R. C. Browning
  Guest, Sir Stanley Machin

TABLE E.—Continued.

Guest, John St. F. Fair
Guest, R. Collet
Guest, H. Williams
Guest, Chevalier E. J. Mazzuchi
Guest, Seymour Hicks
A. M. Matheson
W. E. Merritt

TABLE F.

Stuart S. Mallinson
  Guest, Sir Harold Mackintosh
  Guest, F. Harkness
  Guest S. Wilding Cole
  Guest George Gee
  Guest J. A. Rank
H. G. Vivian
Harold Abrahams
  Guest, E. B. Glanfield.

TABLE G.

Sir Henry J. Buckland
  Guest, Brig.-Gen. C. L. Porter
  Guest, Rev. H. L. Haynes
L. E. L. Donne
J. E. Mills
Douglas R. Jardine
  Guest, Sir Connop Guthrie
  Guest, C. Ogle

TABLE H.

Harry Preston
  Guest, Capt. Pat Thompson
  Guest, W. Millis
  Guest, Comyns Beaumont
R. O. Talbot
Colonel Pack-Beresford
Leslie M. Higham
  Guest, E. M. Loughborough
  Guest, R. Cope
Capt. Nicholls
  Guest, F. F. Cumberworth
D. J. MacMyn

TABLE I.

Colonel Goodbody
  Guest, D. B. Saunderson
  Guest, D. M. Goodbody
Clement V. Paull
  Guest,
A. H. R. Wilson
  Guest, Sir Philip Bowyer-Smyth
  Guest, P. R. Johnson
F. H. Mugliston
W. P. Keith

TABLE K.

Sir Leolin Forestier-Walker
  Guest, Capt Gavin Young
G. L. Weir
A. E. Porritt
  Guest, R. M. Handfield-Jones

TABLE K.—Continued.

R. B. Rees
  Guest, J. P. Hall
  Guest, Commdr. J. Avern
  Guest, C. E. Rualt

TABLE L.

R. C. Sherriff
  Guest, Commdr. H. G. D. Stoker
  Guest, James Agate
W. Ferguson
V. Gordon-Lennox
  Guest,
Howard P. Marshall
  Guest, S. Rogerson

TABLE M.

W. W. Worthington
  Guest, Major J. R. Davison
  Guest, Lt.-Col. Cyril Foley
John Weir
  Guest, H. M. Morris
  Guest, B. E. Tyabji
H. S. Horne
  Guest, W. E. Eborall
H. Cozens-Hardy

TABLE N.

W. W. Wakefield
  Guest,
  Guest, Major T. D. Stoward
R. H. Mallett
M. J. Turnbull
G. F. Earle
Cecil Wray
A. Drew
C. T. Bennett
  Guest, Major C. Perkins
  Guest, B. M. Greenhill

PRESS TABLE I.

Auckland Press (O. S. Hintz)
"Cyclops" (A. C. Ferguson)
Daily Express
Daily Herald
Daily Sketch and *Sunday Graphic*
Evening Standard
New Zealand News (Dr. Harrop)
New Zealand Associated Press
         (T. J. Pemberton)
Press Association

PRESS TABLE II.

Australian Press Association
Central News Agency
Daily Mail (H. J. Henley)
Daily Mirror
Daily Telegraph
Evening News
Morning Post
Sporting Life.
The Times

LEFT: Lunch among the elite at the British Sportsman's Club, before the MCC match at Lord's in 1931.
ABOVE: The seating arrangements.

    The team the MCC put out contained plenty of the game's big guns. There were no less than four England captains – led on this occasion by Lowry's brother-in-law, Percy Chapman, a Grecian figure of English cricket, brilliant batsman and fieldsman, although by 1931 not

Tom leading his team on to the field at Lord's. From left: Ian Cromb, Bill Merritt, Curly Page, Roger Blunt, Tom, Lindsay Weir, Ken James, Jack Mills (rear), Stewie Dempster.

quite the commanding presence of previous years. Alongside Chapman was the angular, austere figure of Douglas Jardine, set to captain England in the forthcoming tests against New Zealand and then, the following year, to be the instigator of Bodyline in Australia, a series that went perilously close to wrecking international cricket. The other skippers were "Farmer" White, left-arm spinner, and Walter Robins, destined to captain England in a series against New Zealand in 1937.

Some of the team had toured New Zealand the previous year. Maurice Allom, considered possibly the most promising pace bowler in England, plus Maurice Turnbull, a Welsh rugby international as well as a sparkling batsman. Pulled into the team late was the only professional selected, Jack Hearne, scorer of 96 first-class hundreds, to bat at No 3. All-rounder Vallance Jupp was another prolific run-scorer, as well as an off-break bowler. Eddie Dawson was the ninth England test player in the team. Only Walter Franklin, the keeper, and Aidan Crawley, the Oxford player who was once 12th man for England, never represented their country. In experience, and first-class (and test) appearances, MCC were light-years ahead of the tourists.

What the MCC may not have reckoned with was that seven of Lowry's men had toured England four years earlier and therefore had the inner confidence of having done it once.

Lowry himself was steeped in English cricket knowledge. Ken James, Stewie Dempster and Bill Merritt were so highly regarded by the English that all subsequently played county cricket. Roger Blunt, alongside Dempster, was a batting star of the tour. Not quite of the same calibre were Curly Page, Jack Kerr, Ron Talbot and "Dad" Weir, but they were fine players, well capable of making an impact. Ian Cromb and Mal Matheson were chosen to open the attack, backed by the leg-spin of Merritt.

The skipper knew he had the full backing of his side. They loved his prescient commentary on the run of play, whether he was on the field or in the pavilion. They knew he was approachable, warm-hearted and kind, but there was also a reserved side to man, perhaps a product of his background on the land. He most certainly refused to suffer fools. On the field he was in charge and everybody knew it. He constantly rang the changes to make things happen, but this hustling also helped him overcome his low boredom threshold. He stayed close to the wicket when fielding – silly mid-off or mid-on, or short leg – all the better to intimidate a batsman and to lead from the front.

It was no surprise to his team-mates when Lowry won the toss (his fourth in four games) on Saturday's opening day at Lord's. "It's just a habit one has," was how he described his penchant for calling correctly. The pitch was good when New Zealand batted, but rain threatened through leaden skies during the morning session. When the visitors went to lunch at 113-4, having lost James, Blunt, Kerr and Page, the downpour arrived so heavily that play was abandoned for the day.

With Sunday cricket still 30 years away, it wasn't until 3.30pm on Monday that play resumed. The conditions were still miserable, a grey, cold, dampish London day enveloping the ground. Unfortunately, matching the conditions was the early demise of New Zealand's star, Dempster, out for 45. The tall, blond Talbot was joined by Lowry. Talbot, a lovely, wristy player, but an inconsistent performer on this tour, was in scintillating form, hitting one six that threatened to equal Albert Trott's record as the only player to hit a ball clean over the pavilion at Lord's. Talbot's shot of at least 125 metres hit the pavilion roof before rebounding back into the hands of Robins.

Ron Talbot smashed a never-to-be-forgotten six at Lord's.

The skipper's batting reputation was also based on hitting. He was a driver and a hooker, with a preference for on-side play. So powerful was his shot-making that in his county cricket days, a Sussex slow bowler being flayed to all parts of the field was heard to say: "Anywhere sir, hit 'em anywhere, but for the Lord's sake not straight back at me."

Lowry could be a bit shaky in defence and while his long experience gave him the guile and skill to keep out the best bowlers, he tended to use attack as the best means of countering danger. When he strode to the wicket, muttering about the dismissal of the outgoing batsman, his team knew he would use every resource in his repertoire, even including his body to absorb a short-pitched ball, to stop a batting slump setting in.

The crowd at Lord's that day saw a virtuoso Lowry display. Talbot scored a handsome 66 in just 50 minutes, but that was soon cast into the shadows alongside the dominance and magnificence of Lowry's batting.

After a watchful opening, he was smartly into his stride against the attack of Allom, White, Jupp, Robins and Hearne. Casting aside any brother-in-law camaraderie, Chapman set a leg-theory field to exploit the turning ball from Jupp.

But Lowry couldn't be tamed. He dealt with the wily Jupp's leg-theory in much the same way as Don Bradman endeavoured to counter the lethal Larwood a year or so later. Jupp would pitch his off-spinners on the leg stump for the benefit of the ring of leg fieldsman, but the burly Lowry simply moved to the leg side, hitting against the spin through point and cover. The method was risky, but Lowry played with such confidence and skill that at no stage did he appear in danger of losing his wicket. This was an utterly ruthless performance by Lowry and while he deliberately and effectively dealt with Jupp, he set about destroying the length of any of the bowlers in Chapman's line-up as soon as they arrived at the bowling crease.

Lowry scored 52 runs out of 66 in 80 minutes and then added the 48 needed for his century in close to a run a minute. He raced to his century by stumps. There was just one chance, when he was 60. When play ended on the second day with New Zealand 301-9 – Lowry 101 not out – the match, with only a day remaining, seemed all but over and heading for another one of cricket's inevitable draws.

Cricket, as they say, can be a funny game. On day three Lowry declared at the overnight score. Then the real fun started. What Lord's witnessed on May 19 rocked the English cricket world. Lowry and Talbot had given the tourists a respectable score, but now the drama quotient climbed several notches.

The powerful MCC batting side had to reckon with Ian ("Cranky") Cromb, a brisk, medium-pace bowler with the ability to make the ball zip off the pitch and hurry a batsman. On this final day's play and on a reasonable batting pitch, he got the ball to move both ways and immediately had MCC reeling. By the time they were 41-6, the Cantabrian had taken 5-15, impressing his own side, but equally Douglas Jardine, who fought to give his side some respectability. Jardine batted patiently, displaying a sound technique for an unbeaten 62. He said of Cromb: "He's a really good bowler, who can make the ball hit the bat before the bat has time to hit the ball."

Cromb's outstanding bowling (6-46) was matched by equally brilliant fielding, with Page the standout, snaffling three fine catches in the slips, including a low left-handed effort to dismiss Chapman first ball.

MCC scored just 132, and were all out after lunch, but still there was no sign that the match would end in anything other than a draw.

By 1931, the leadership of the visiting skipper had become a subject of admiration and considerable talk throughout England. It was regarded as original, unorthodox, occasionally eccentric. From boy to man he'd been in charge of his sports teams – from Okawa to Heretaunga, from Christ's to Cambridge, from Wellington to New Zealand. Under his captaincy, bowlers needed to hit their straps pretty smartly because he had no compunction in shuffling them with alarming rapidity. Equally he could demand a long stint at the crease as Cromb once discovered (constantly demanding the skipper bowl him, he found, much to his chagrin, that he was forced to bowl 20 consecutive overs).

Lowry's players, from time to time, may have tut-tutted about his instinctive approach, but his moves frequently worked and they would throw back their heads in glee and wonderment at his insight. Up close, at silly mid-off or short leg, his laser-like detection of a player's weakness enabled him to orchestrate his moves. He flew solo in captaincy, needing little consultation, leading with an autocratic "Let's get it done" and "I'll show you the way" attitude.

When Lowry asked his brother-in-law to follow on, there were just three hours remaining in the match. Chapman called for the heavy roller, hoping that anything left in the pitch for the bowlers would be flattened out, enabling his batting side to comfortably play out the time.

This move by Chapman was later criticised as, in fact, not being helpful, presumably because it may have assisted in breaking up the pitch. Given the quality of the Lord's pitch, as it was then, there seems little reason for any excuse at all, the heavy roller or inept batting.

When first innings top-scorer Jardine walked out with the most prolific scorer of the season to date, Jack Hearne, all seemed set for a meandering run towards stumps. Lowry had other ideas.

First he had to withstand a withering, displeased stare from Cromb, because after an opening over from Matheson, it wasn't Cromb who was in Lowry's sights for the opening over from the opposite end. Cromb, with his memorable six-wicket bag in the first innings, must surely have thought it was his right to have a crack at dismissing the MCC for a second time. Instead he had to busy himself with keeping warm, wrapped in two sweaters (as all players were) against the bitterly cold conditions.

Instead Lowry tossed the ball to leg-spinner Merritt, a move described as impulsive – he had told no-one of his plan of action.

In his book on the tour, Budge Hintz describes how Hearne at the striker's end turned to Page in the slips with an air of wonder: "This fellow with the new ball! Does he expect him to turn it?" Hintz went on: "Merritt supplied the answer in his second over. A ball pitched just outside the Middlesex professional's off stump, and he politely ignored what he thought was a leg-spinner. But it was Merritt's wrong-un and a second later Hearne was looking back disconsolately at his middle stump, which was leaning back at a rakish angle."

It took another 60 years before another New Zealand captain, Martin Crowe, would gamble so insightfully, making his team highly competitive by opening the bowling with another spinner, this time an offie, Dipak Patel, in the 1992 World Cup.

Douglas Jardine, top scorer in both innings for the MCC. This was only months before the history-making Bodyline series.

The procession was on. Blunt replaced Matheson, and he and Merritt destroyed the MCC second innings. Dawson played too soon at a ball that beat him in the air – caught Merritt bowled Blunt. Crawley made a half-volley into a yorker, hitting across a straight ball, and was bowled by Merritt. Desperation had yet to set in, but it wasn't far off.

Turnbull scored two off his first ball and off the next was brilliantly stumped by James from Merritt's bowling. Then Chapman arrived to break the pair of spectacles, but first ball he was once again picked up at slip by Page, giving Merritt his fourth wicket and Chapman an ignominious record if ever there was one – a first-ball duck in both innings for the England captain. Lowry must surely have proffered up a wry smile to his brother-in-law.

Lowry got further into the act with a fine leaping left-handed catch at mid-off to get rid of Jupp and give Merritt wicket No 5. Now the heavy roller effect came into play when Jardine, MCC's last realistic chance of saving the game, was bowled by a shooter from Blunt for

Bill Merritt opened the bowling and spun New Zealand to a famous victory.

19, the top score again, and the only double-figures in the second innings. Robins tried to cover-drive a leg-break from Merritt and was bowled without scoring, and White holed out to mid-off off the same bowler before Blunt wrapped up the innings by getting the wicket of Allom.

In just one hour and five minutes Lowry and his men had dealt "a sledge-hammer blow to the prestige of the Premier club" by bowling them out for 48. The heroes of the second innings were the leg-spinning duo, Merritt 7-28 and Blunt 3-13.

The stunned English press was in ecstatic mood for the tourists when the morning newspapers hit the streets. Pelham Warner, in the *Morning Post*, said: "The victory at the headquarters of cricket will add immensely to the tourists' growing reputation." The *Daily Mail* carped at the MCC with: "The New Zealand bowlers completely fooled the batsmen. The wicket was little different from that on which the visitors scored 302 runs." And the *Daily Telegraph* said: "A surprise may be in store for the cricketing world when the New Zealanders play the test match. The visitors' youth and zest are creating a strong impression."

Back in New Zealand, editorial writers couldn't hold back. One wrote: "A gasp of surprise and delight has gone up from New Zealand today and for a little while many men (women, of course, take little interest in cricket) have forgotten the iron face of the time. On the historic ground at Lord's, the New Zealand cricket team has crushingly defeated a strong MCC side, dismissing them for 48 runs in the second innings. 'Where are your All Blacks now?' one can imagine an enthusiastic cricketer asking... More than any previous success, this puts New Zealand cricket on the map."

Much like Sunday cricket, the pyjama game, and batting helmets, this amazing victory was decades away from the presence of commercialism that helped usher in Man of the Match awards, presentation medals, cheques and sponsors' products. But, in a game where Cromb and Merritt would have been worthy winners, Tom Lowry stood out for laying the foundation with his first innings century and then, by a stroke of genius, introducing Merritt to bowl out the MCC when they followed on. There was no happier man in England that night.

The MCC dinner had been held at Lord's on the Monday night of the match, at the end of day two, and on a free night back at their hotel, Tom was able to enjoy one or two whiskies and a game of poker.

2d. Lord's CC Ground

M.C.C. v. NEW ZEALAND.

SATURDAY, MONDAY & TUESDAY, MAY 16, 18, 19, 1931.

NEW ZEALAND.		First Innings.		Second Innings.
1 C. S. Dempster	Wellington	c and b White	45	
*2 K. C. James	Wellington	l b w, b Allom	1	
3 R. C. Blunt	Otago	b Robins	5	
4 J. L. Kerr	Canterbury	c Dawson, b Jupp	24	
5 M. L. Page	Canterbury	c White, b Jupp	14	
6 R. O Talbot	Canterbury	c Crawley, b White	66	
†7 T. C. Lowry	Wellington	not out	101	
8 I. B. Cromb	Canterbury	c White, b Robins	8	
9 G. L. Weir	Auckland	st Franklin, b Jupp	12	
10 W. E. Merritt	Canterbury	c Franklin, b White	15	
11 A. M. Matheson	Auckland	not out	5	
		B , l-b 6, w , n-b	6	B , l-b , w , n-b ,
*Innings closed.		Total	*302	Total

FALL OF THE WICKETS.

1-9	2-28	3 77	4 83	5-158	6-163	7-190	8-262	9 291	10-
1-	2-	3-	4-	5-	6-	7-	8-	9-	10-

ANALYSIS OF BOWLING.

Name.	O.	M.	R.	W.	Wd.	N-b.	O.	M.	R.	W.	Wd.	N-b.
			1st Innings.						2nd Innings.			
Allom	19	2	57	1	...	...	...	...	...	...	...	...
Hearne	8	5	17	0	...	...	...	...	...	...	...	...
Robins	20	1	50	2	...	...	...	...	...	...	...	...
Jupp	31	3	106	3	...	...	...	...	...	...	...	...
White	28	7	66	3	...	...	...	...	...	...	...	...

M. C. C.		First Innings.		Second Innings.	
1 E. W. Dawson		c Lowry, b Cromb	1	c Merritt, b Blunt	2
2 Hearne, J. W.		b Cromb	12	b Merritt	0
3 A. M. Crawley		c Page, b Matheson	0	b Merritt	1
4 D. R. Jardine		not out	62	b Blunt	19
5 M. J. Turnbull		l b w, b Cromb	0	st James, b Merritt	2
6 V. W. C. Jupp		c and b Cromb	12	c Lowry b Merritt	5
†7 A. P. F. Chapman		c Page, b Cromb	0	c Page, b Merritt	0
8 R. W. V. Robins		c Blunt, b Matheson	16	b Merritt	0
9 J. C. White		c Page, b Cromb	17	not out	7
*10 W. B. Franklin		l b w, b Merritt	2	c Kerr, b Merritt	2
11 M. J. C. Allom		c Kerr, b Merritt	0	c Kerr, b Blunt	9
		B 6, l-b 3, w , n-b 1,	10	B , l-b 1, w , n-b ,	1
		Total	132	Total	48

FALL OF THE WICKETS.

1 3	2 6	3 20	4 21	5-41	6 41	7-67	8 125	9-132	10-132
1-4	2-15	3-18	4-20	5-20	6-28	7-30	8 30	9 32	10 48

ANALYSIS OF BOWLING.

Name.	O.	M.	R.	W.	Wd.	N-b.	O.	M.	R.	W.	Wd.	N-b.
			1st Innings.						2nd Innings.			
Matheson	11	4	16	2	...	...	3	1	6	0	...	...
Cromb	23	7	46	6	...	...	...	...	...	...	...	...
Merritt	17.5	4	49	2	...	1	9	3	28	7	...	...
Blunt	4	1	11	0	...	...	6.1	1	13	3	...	...

Umpires—Morton and Hardstaff.   Scorers—Mavins and Ferguson.
The figures on the Scoring Board show the batsmen in.
Play commences at 11.30 each day.

Luncheon at 1.30.   *Wicket-keeper.
†Captain.
Stumps drawn 1st and 2nd days at 6.30, 3rd day at 6.

[TEA INTERVAL—There will probably be a Tea Interval at **4.30-4.45** but it will depend on the state of the game.

NEW ZEALAND WON THE TOSS.

SCORES FROM OTHER GROUNDS.

OVAL—Surrey v. Hampshire	Hampshire 127—0
NOTTINGHAM—Nottinghamshire v. Northamptonshire	Notts 132—2
WORCESTER—Worcestershire v. Lancashire	Lancashire 9—1
LEEDS—Yorkshire v. Warwickshire	Yorkshire won by an innings & 25 runs
LEICESTER—Leicestershire v. Essex	Leicester 96—5
DERBY—Derbyshire v. Kent	Derby 127—6
HOVE—Sussex v. Gloucestershire	Sussex 93—0
CAMBRIDGE—Cambridge University Middlesex	Middlesex 135—7

The Lowry late cut. Normally a hard-hitting driver, Tom could play deftly when required.

The skipper, a man devoid of self-aggrandisement, could now reflect on the accumulated knowledge and experience that allowed him to arrive in this position of superior cricket captain, leader of men and psychologist. The endless cricket summers in Hawke's Bay, his days as an outstanding schoolboy leader and big hitter, his early struggles at Cambridge, the lessons learned from his Somerset captain, the exposure to the best players in the game and the numerous tours – including, of all things, a colonial playing for the MCC – had given him a standing in the game in his home country, and his status and influence had helped gain acceptance by England for the initial New Zealand tours there.

To cap it off, there were the influences of his two brothers-in-law, equally outstanding international sportsmen who helped to provide an unusual triumvirate of sporting endeavour.

That glowing night he might have equally been content back home on his property, tending to his land and his stock, or watching out for the quickest of his foals flicking across the paddocks. But this big, dominating, no-nonsense man had shown that it was possible for the Lilliputians of the game to truly punch above their weight.

2. Origins

Forty years after the end of Tom Lowry's career, cricket's bible, *Wisden*, mistakenly still referred to his birthplace as Wellington, New Zealand. *Wisden*, like others, had been lured into a deception that made New Zealand's capital a convenient "in" for Tom to qualify to play county cricket for Somerset, also a region with a town of Wellington, but that's where the similarity ended.

Wellington, New Zealand, southern hemisphere – wind-blown, picturesque, 300,000 population. Wellington, Somerset, England, northern hemisphere – a small country town of just 13,000.

Thomas Coleman Lowry, like his father before him, was born on the family property, Okawa, at Fernhill. A small service village, Fernhill lies 20km south-west of Napier and 10km west of Hastings. Today, heading from Napier you arrive at Fernhill and then swing right up Taihape Road for another 7.5km before arriving at a low stone wall, signalling your arrival at Okawa. This pocket of Hawke's Bay farmland still bears a resemblance to its original grassland. It is distinctly sheep and cattle-grazing territory, unlike a good part of the countryside, now devoted to the growing of grapes as Hawke's Bay has progressed into a major wine-producing region.

Fernhill in 1898, the year of Tom's birth, comprised a local store, which also supplied postal services, including money-order and telephone conveniences. While the local store was no doubt a regular stopping point for supplies and conversation, the Maori pa, a church (for weekly services) and the Fernhill Hotel, which Tom and his siblings were given strict instructions to avoid, were equally vital community amenities.

The two-storeyed wooden hotel stood out, with three sitting rooms, a dining table capable of seating 18 guests, a billiard room with a full-sized Burroughs and Watt billiard table, and several single and double guest bedrooms. The bar was well-stocked with the best brands of spirits, liqueurs, wines (although certainly not with the reputation, quality or variety Hawke's Bay currently produces) and a Napier brew of ale. These temptations were no doubt the reason for the Lowry ban on the hotel, although Tom and his brothers devised ways of circumventing the "no-go" rule.

Tom's paternal grandfather, Thomas, settled at Okawa in 1852, but not before exploring other parts of New Zealand in search of the most suitable farmland. Thomas had arrived at Auckland on the barque Ralph Bernal on June 28, 1846, after a journey via the Cape of Good Hope that took more than six months. Wasting no time, he immediately set off to explore Northland and bought 23 cows, some calves and 300 ewes and lambs. These were grazed for him while he then checked out the South Island. He lived for some time in Nelson, and also Wellington, then showed an interest in settling permanently in the Wairarapa. In

1849, he bought some land at Lake Rotoaira, south of Taupo. Two years later he leased land in Cheviot, Canterbury, where the Lowry Peaks still bear his name. But momentously for future Lowry generations, it was from his North Island property that he made a trip with Maori guides into Hawke's Bay, travelling the route over the Gentle Annie track that is now the Taihape-Napier road.

The Hawke's Bay freehold property he bought from Maori (before the Maori Land Act) was fern country, like a good part of Hawke's Bay. In his book *Tutira*, Herbert Guthrie-Smith wrote of his own station: "On eighteen out of twenty thousand acres it is no exaggeration to say that the surface had to be stamped, jammed, hauled, murdered into grass." Of Hawke's Bay he said: "I can hardly think of any settler of early times who had not been at one time or another on his last legs."

This, too, was the case for Thomas Lowry. Once the fern and scrub clearance had taken place, the terrain revealed itself as first-class, summer dry land, suitable for grain growing and sheep farming. An early discovery on the land was an iron spring and so the property was named Okawa, meaning "bitter water".

Thomas was born in Crosby-on-Eden, Carlisle, Cumberland, England, in 1814, the second son of yet another Thomas, The Rev Lowry DD (Doctors of Divinity were granted by universities and conferred on a religious scholar of distinction and standing). Well-educated, a classical scholar with a BA at Christ's College, Cambridge, and someone ready for a challenge, Thomas fitted historian James Belich's "pulled" category of "Europeans" heading to the new world in the first half of the 19th century, as distinct from the "pushed" category. New Zealand agents such as the Wakefield brothers were advocating for removal to the "Britain of the South" in which "British class distinctions were preserved and where industrious artisans and farmers could more easily work their way to prosperity and respectability".

There was one other reason why Thomas may have been "pulled". It was revealed in a letter to a Miss Storey of Bishop Yards, Penrith.

1843

My Dear Miss Storey
As no opportunity of seeing you is likely to present itself shortly the only mode of addressing you is by letter. I write then to ask you to become my wife and in case you do not accept my offer, I shall rely on you not proclaiming it to the world...

It has long been my intention to quit my native land to exchange it for another, where I could amass a large fortune, for New Zealand where the climate is so beautiful, free from extremes of heat and cold, and nature is always bathed in beauty. I am possessed of a thousand pounds but at the death of my mother (which I trust is far off, but I fear is too near) I succeed to an independent estate...

You will perhaps be kind enough to favour me with an answer about the latter by the end of next week...

In case you decline my service, pray do not hold me up to ridicule...

Yours sincerely
Thos. Lowry

Unfortunately for Thomas, he was turned down by Miss Storey and it was nearly 20 years before he eventually found his wife. As revealed in his marriage proposal letter, Thomas was blessed with some monetary means and access to more. Several times in his early New Zealand days he borrowed from his sisters back in the United Kingdom and recorded that the interest on this was being sent home. These borrowings helped him develop his New Zealand land ownership. Thomas had other gifts as well, with, in particular, a special facility to inspire confidence in Maori. Writing home to a nephew in his early New Zealand days, he showed a respect and affection for Maori that was later to be reciprocated.

Auckland
April 7th, 1847

My Dear Joe,
I am happy to tell you that I approve greatly of the choice I have made of New Zealand. It is a fine country and very healthy. I only reached Auckland in the month of August last, and since my arrival in the country I have never been long stationary in the same place. I expect in the course of the next few months to be finally settled in the country. There has been considerable difficulty in getting upon land, not withstanding that the natives are all very anxious to have white settlers amongst them. A code of regulations, however, is about being drawn up, which will enable people to settle where they like. I have got a good many cattle and sheep, which are being kept for me in the country. I believe I have three and twenty cows, besides a good many calves, and about three hundred ewes and lambs together. The natives are a very lively set of people and the best tempered fellows I ever saw. They are quite civilised, and are working by hundreds on the roads and many are putting up stone buildings for Government.

They are quite an agricultural people and produce vast quantities of potatoes and pigs. They have a singular custom of rubbing noses with each other. You would be amused if you saw them nosing each other. If two friends have not met each other for some time, they will rub noses and sob for half an hour. They generally sob and shed tears while they nose. I have seen girls sitting in the middle of the street, rubbing noses and making a sad moaning for a long time.

The climate of New Zealand is really beautiful and the country with all its advantages cannot fail, I think, to become great and prosperous. It is really wonderful how cattle and sheep thrive here. All the English fruits grow remarkably well in New Zealand. There are not finer apples and pears grown in the world, perhaps, than at places called the "Bay of Islands". There is much more fruit produced at the Bay of Islands than at other settlements as it is of older standing. The other places have only sprung up within the last few years. Oranges, I believe, have not been produced in New Zealand yet, but if they grow in Devonshire, in England, they might surely be grown in northern parts of New Zealand. I purpose [sic] going on a journey shortly into the interior of the country. There are some boiling springs at a place called "Rotorua", at no very great distance from Auckland. I purpose [sic] going to Rotorua first.

The most powerful chief in New Zealand, called Te Whero Whero, has been in Auckland during the last few weeks. He is a nice looking old man, with a very mild expression of countenance. From his appearance, one would not say that such a man could ever have delighted in shedding blood – yet this very person has no doubt eaten many, very many, of his fellow creatures. The New Zealanders are all the most dreadful cannibals, but since the introduction of Christianity amongst them, they have laid aside the dreadful propensity, and are patterns of good conduct to their white brethren.

And, now, my dear boy, I must wish you good-bye. I shall hope to hear from you. I hope that your sister Jane, and Mr and Mrs Hudson and your Aunt are all well.

Believe me to be

Your affectionate Uncle,
Thos. Lowry

Thomas' arrival in New Zealand could not have been better timed. The wars of the 1840s had petered out and a period of stability between Maori and Pakeha existed from 1847 to 1860. Military posts in Napier and Taradale were useful in maintaining a peaceful co-existence at least until the late 1860s, when Te Kooti waged guerrilla campaigns through a number of North Island regions, including Hawke's Bay, and the Hau Hau uprising of 1868 when, for safety reasons, the women at Okawa were forced off the property for more than a year. The late 1840s and early 1850s also coincided with the golden age of Pakeha land buying, when Governor Grey and his land buyer, Donald McLean, purchased 32.6 million acres, just under half the whole country, at an average of less than a halfpenny per acre.

The first white settlers in Hawke's Bay had been whalers – rough-hewn types, fond of rum but responsible for setting up the first European industry. Then came the missionaries and traders, before the real developers of the region, the farmers, arrived.

In 1849, James Henry Northwood and Henry Stokes Tiffen rolled into Pourerere with 3000 merinos to graze on a 40,000-acre spread, the first Hawke's Bay sheep station. Soon others followed. They became the famous names in the region – the Herberts, Russells, Ormonds and, of course, Lowrys.

By buying Okawa, Thomas, at last, was able to fully put into practice his long-held ambition to farm the land in a way that reflected his interest in sheep and cattle, nurtured years earlier in pastoral Cumberland. Okawa at that stage consisted of 10,500 acres (bought for £800). As well as Okawa, he acquired another 5500 acres, probably including the Muriwhenua block and possibly Pukehamoana. The land choice was discerning and far-sighted. It had plentiful water, natural boundaries, dry hills for the winter, heavy hills for hoggets in winter, flats for growing oats and heavy low country for fattening bullocks and growing out young stock. Thomas' foresight cannot be underestimated. All these years later, Okawa is still owned by a Lowry and is a property that has produced not only prize-winning sheep and cattle, but leading horse progeny. It is an estate with its own cricket ground and two tennis courts. In human terms it has produced outstanding New Zealanders in the fields of sport, farming, horse ownership, administration and business. This is not to forget the considerable wealth for the family and the country that has been generated by Okawa.

In 1862, many years after his initial rejection, Thomas found his bride, marrying Maria Beamish, from a family he knew while in Wellington. Four children followed. The first was Georgina (Lizzie), then a son and heir, Thomas Henry (Harry or TH), born on the estate in 1865, followed by Mary and Alice. Thomas continued to develop the property and, with other land interests taxing his capacity to cope, more help was needed. Eventually Maria's brother, Nathaniel (Nat), was brought out from England to manage the estate. By the 1870s it was carrying 21,000 sheep and most of the land had been bought and the necessary leases renewed. In addition, Thomas imported berries, nectarines, gum trees, oaks and poplars from Australia and England, as well as ducks, turkeys and geese.

Maria played a major part in the running of the station, taking over the special care of the bees. She also made the hop beer and the sausages and just for good measure killed the rats as well. Maria was also a fearless horsewoman, something that became a tradition among the female riders at Okawa.

Morning prayers were an institution, with everyone assembling at 8am, after responding to the ringing of the ship's bell. Sunday school for all the children was held on Sunday afternoon, while periodically, when the local clergyman paid his rotating station visit, a service would be held in the homestead. This was generally followed by a cricket match.

In 1880, when TH was attending Christ's College in Christchurch, he was summoned back to Napier to see his very ill father, dying at "The Spa" in Taupo. Thomas failed to rally and at age 15 TH became the inheritor of the property.

Management, in the meantime, fell to Maria's brother, Nat, under the direction of the trustees of the estate. Thomas had long cherished an ambition to take his son back to Crosby-on-Eden and also for him to follow in his footsteps at Cambridge. This task was now undertaken by Maria. Together with other family members, Maria and TH travelled to England where TH attended Cirencester Agricultural College and Jesus College, Cambridge, staying for six years.

Back in New Zealand, TH had a burning desire to fully take over the property. While he still had the sure hands of Nat Beamish to support him and head shepherd Johnson to show him the fine art of the care of sheep, the benefit of youthful enterprise gave TH the chance to take the property and business to its next stage of development. Thomas had established Okawa and acquired the leases of Kawera and Pukehaumoana (neighbouring properties), but TH was even more ambitious in moving to expand the property.

Although by now a prominent Hawke's Bay landowner and farmer, TH's marriage to Helen (Marsie) Watt in 1897 added in more ways than one to the well-being of the Lowry family and its future generations. TH met Helen on the road to Waikoko to play tennis and in a later discussion expressed his conviction that "when it came to beauty, the Watt girls took a lot of beating".

Helen's father, James Watt, who died prematurely in 1879, aged 45, was then widely believed to be one of the richest men in New Zealand, a fortune acquired by bringing the first steam boats to New Zealand. These he used to ship in supplies to Hawke's Bay from Auckland and then to export the Hawke's Bay wool clip. Watt also owned one of Hawke's Bay's largest sheep stations, Longlands, plus land at Kohimarama in Auckland, where he trained his horses on the beach. This racing interest also led to him becoming the first president of the Auckland Racing Club.

Left with a very large inheritance, and four children under seven, his widow, Hannah, wasted no time in re-marrying a year later, to another entrepreneur and pillar of Hawke's Bay society, James Coleman. A private merchant-banker, Coleman retired at 45 due to ill-health.

An irrepressible, thick-set man with an enormous walrus moustache, each day he would descend the Napier hill to harass his solicitor, and then proceed to dish out the same treatment to his banker. Thereafter this ebullient character would retire for the afternoon (and frequently most evenings) to the Hawke's Bay Club. This was Tom's step-grandfather and the person from whom he inherited his second name.

Like Tom's siblings in the next generation, the Watt-Coleman children married – as society at that time would have judged – rather well. While only son Eddie, who was to play a significant monetary part in Tom's future, remained a bachelor until well into his 40s, all three girls found partners of note. Helen, of course, married TH Lowry, and Florence married Robert Baden-Powell's (of scouting fame) brother, Francis. It was middle daughter Gertrude who made the most spectacular catch.

While her brother Eddie was at Cambridge University, he became pals with a charming, good-looking action-man by the name of Ewart Grogan. Grogan was one of 21 children of Queen Victoria's surveyor-general. At 21, he served in Cecil Rhodes' personal escort in the 1896 Matabele war. To recover from many ailments sustained in this conflict and at the invitation of Eddie Watt, he took a sea voyage to New Zealand and promptly fell in love with Eddie's sister Gertrude.

In *Lost Lion of the Empire* (the Grogan biography), Gertrude was described as "a tall girl, almost as tall as Grogan, with soft blue eyes and thick lustrous, brown hair, but what attracted Grogan most was her booming laugh, which was infectious, her serenity and the exceptionally warm heart she had inherited from her Mother".

While a guest of the Watt-Colemans, Grogan decided to broach the subject of marriage with James Coleman. Now the trustee of the sizeable inheritance left to the Watt children, Coleman wanted to know Grogan's prospects, but was set back by Grogan's reply. Inspired by Rhodes' dream of a Cape to Cairo railway and telegraph – an imperial highway through Africa - and the fact that no man had surveyed the whole route, Grogan declared his intention to make his mark by undertaking the first south to north traverse of Africa.

In *Lost Lion of the Empire*, Coleman shuffled.

"I can only presume you are trying to be funny. If so I do not appreciate it."

"Oh no sir, certainly not. I am quite serious, never more so."

"Then you must be a fool. You mean to say you really contemplate crossing the entire continent of Africa. My good man, do you realise what that would mean?"

"Perfectly...if I succeed I should hope to have proved myself worthy of your step-daughter."

A few days later Grogan said goodbye and left for home.

Later described as one of the most swashbuckling and controversial figures of colonial history, Grogan completed his trek from Cape Town to Cairo and in early 1900 returned to London a hero. In October, having proved his mettle, he married Gertrude, together with a dowry that was estimated to be between £2 million and £10 million, or even more. While the Grogans spent a good part of their lives in Africa, Tom and his siblings had contact with them in London after World War I, affectionately referring to Grogan as "Grog". There were also some family reservations about their contact with Grogan because of his extra-marital activities. Unbeknown for some time by Gertrude, he had fathered children by at least two other women.

Back in Hawke's Bay, Gertrude's sister, Marsie, was now married to TH (and presumably delivering a similar dowry to Gertrude) and they set about producing their family. Thomas Coleman (Tom or TC), was the first born, in 1898, followed by James North (Jim) 1900, Ralph Henry Watt (Ralph) 1901, Gertrude Helen Hudson (Beet) 1902 and Marion Grogan 1904.

The beginning of the 20th century proved a boom time in New Zealand, with prosperity tied to the exploitation of areas like Hawke's Bay's grasslands into wool, meat and skins through the grazing of sheep, and butter, cheese and meat by grazing cattle.

Okawa, with 20,000 acres, was regarded as one of the finest properties of the district, with the homestead now developed and surrounded by beautiful grounds. There were 35,000 lincoln sheep and lambs shorn annually and there was a herd of shorthorn cattle numbering 550, many of exceptional value. TH was also breeding pedigree shorthorn bulls for sale, while there was a large demand for his lincoln rams and his stock of breeding ewes. Added to this were his 80 horses, many pure bred from blood mares and sires. His father's vision of introducing the best breed of cattle, horses and sheep into the district was now paying dividends.

In partnership with his brother-in-law, Eddie Watt, TH also expanded into Australia, buying property in New South Wales.

TH was strong, fit and active, and alongside his farming and business enterprises he extended his not inconsiderable sports prowess. His education years had given him versatility across a wide range of sports and he excelled at cricket, rugby, golf, tennis and racing. On his return to Okawa from Cambridge, he represented Hawke's Bay at cricket in the late 1880s and early 1890s. Hawke's Bay at this stage qualified as one of New Zealand's first-class cricket sides, being granted that status at the formation of the association in 1882, just a few years before TH's return from Cambridge. This first-class status continued until 1920-21, when the Plunket Shield competition changed from a challenge system to a league system, so TH's appearances for Hawke's Bay were regarded as first-class.

TH was an all-rounder, described as a stylish batsman. According to Hawke's Bay cricket historian Frank Cane, he was handicapped (as were a few other players) by his farming commitments, which led to an inability to practise. If TH couldn't get the necessary practice to spend long periods at the batting crease, he made up for it with his bowling. In the 1891-92 season, he appeared on the province's honours board, taking 40 wickets in all senior matches at the astoundingly economic average of just 5.7.

There is no doubt Tom's later cricket success could be attributed to the love of the game instilled by his father. So enamoured was TH with cricket that on taking over Okawa he promptly had prepared a cricket ground, suitable for local "test" matches. Lined with poplars, it had many wider uses than just cricket, including hunts, girl guides, pony club and family picnics. To be fair, TH also had altruistic reasons for the ground. These were the days when the shearing was done with blades, so the shearers were encamped for long periods and the ground could be utilised for periods of recreation.

"The Grove", as it was known, was decidedly rustic, with an old shed for the pavilion, but it was also adorned with a picket fence and a scoreboard. Coconut matting was used for the pitch, its tightness or looseness altered where necessary for home side advantage. This fiddling with the matting was to become even more fine-tuned when Tom and some of his illustrious cricket friends appeared on the Grove. Meanwhile, fieldsmen needed to be ever-vigilant of cow dung and sheep poop.

A "Grove" score sheet survives from 1889 with TH in all his pomp (and presumably with the matting suitably doctored) taking six wickets, five bowled. This was a match between Okawa and the Hastings Butterflies, a team that appears to have fluttered off the cricket stage with no other record of engagement.

It was a handy side including as opening batsman one of Hawke's Bay's most noted cricket identities, Heathcote Williams (a Hawke's Bay orchardist), plus Jack Taiaroa (one of the first Maori solicitors, a representative cricketer and holder of a national long jump title) and other Bay representatives. The fact that TH and Heathcote Williams were engaging at this stage was significant for the game in the province because on numerous occasions later they joined together as benefactors, particularly in the area of supporting the introduction of professional coaches.

TH Lowry, who became a generous benefactor for cricket and, later, one of the big figures in the horse-racing industry.

If TH was mild-mannered – the strong, silent type – wife Marsie (her affectionate name acquired through her love of marzipan) was the opposite. Here was the classic matriarch, ruling and controlling. Some said TH made the bullets and Marsie fired them – "she did the talking for everyone". Grandson Tom Junior remembered her as very kind, but knew that other people were frightened of her.

In later life Tom Junior met somebody who said: "I can remember your grandmother when I was a travelling salesman, so I called at Okawa and she said, 'What do you want?' I replied I had something to sell and she said, 'Well, I need a hand. Come and sit with me on the verandah.' After making lavender bags for five hours I decided I wasn't going to sell her anything."

This was a formidable woman who knew what she wanted. An inveterate traveller with wide connections, particularly in the United Kingdom, she gave the Lowrys their foothold into the upper echelons of English society while they played sport and attended university. She later became rather large (her mother reached 17st, as did her sister, Gertrude), which may have led to health complications. On a trip to Tahiti and in terrible pain from gallstones, she was reputed to have died and legend has it that she had a spiritual experience that "if she gave up considering herself and served others she would live". From that moment, Marsie spent her entire life doing kindly acts while spending her money endeavouring to help others not as fortunate as herself – soldiers, the blind, the poor and the sick.

So generous was Marsie that on one occasion she lent her grand piano for a worthy cause, only to be stunned on her next trip to town to find the piano as the first prize in a raffle. She furiously demanded an explanation. Back came the answer: "Don't worry, Mrs Lowry, we've got you on the winning ticket."

Much of her good work revolved around her activities with the Red Cross and the Order of St John. She became the Dominion president of the New Zealand Red Cross and Dame of Grace of the Order of St John. The lavender bags weren't wasted. During World War I, she,

Match played at _Okawa_ on _8 Feb_ 1889

Hastings Butterflies 1st Innings.

Order of going in.	BATSMEN'S NAMES.	RUNS AS SCORED.	HOW OUT.	BOWLER.	TOTAL.
1	Williams	1434432231313	c & b Lowry	Lowry	34
2	Loughman	451264	Run out	Jamieson	22
3	Brathwaite	11	c Sanders	Lowry	2
4	Fenwick		Bowled	Lowry	0
5	Lawson	143	Bowled	Lowry	8
6	Lawson	311/1334	Bowled	Walsh	17
7	Gordon b	3131	Bowled	Lowry	8
8	Fitzroy	1133/111	do	do	11
9	Carter 2	1842	Bowled	Lowry	7
10	Mylford		Not out		0
11	Potts	21	Caught Walsh	Jamieson	2
		Byes 1822/222			14
		Leg byes 2			2
		Wide balls			
		No balls			
				Total of 1st Innings	128

Runs at the fall of each wicket.	1 for 42	2 for 59	3 for 63	4 for 68	5 for 74	6 for 94	7 for 100	8 for	9 for 122	10 for 128

BOWLER.	ANALYSIS OF BOWLING.—Number of "Overs," and Runs made from each Bowler.																		No Balls.	Wide Balls.
	1	2	3	4	5	6	7	8	9	10	11	12	13	14	15	16	17	18		
Jamieson																				

NAME OF BOWLER.	No. of No Balls.	No. of Wide Balls.	Total Runs.	Maiden Overs.	No. of Wickets Bowled.	No. of Balls.	NAME OF BOWLER.	No of No Balls.	No. of Wide Balls.	Total Runs.	Maiden Overs.	No. of Wickets Bowled.	No. of Balls.
Duke													

THE REGISTERED SCORE SHEET

Tom's father, TH, with a six-wicket haul on "the Grove" at Okawa, leading his side against the Hastings Butterflies.

along with TH, financed the Lowry Hut in France, a recreational facility for soldiers (more later of another Lowry Hut, in World War II), and much of the lavender bag production finished up in France. All this industry and philanthropy resulted in an OBE for Marsie in 1918.

Marsie was also influential in the building of one of the most impressive houses at Okawa. The original house at Okawa was a small cottage at the end of the current garden, but when Maria arrived as Thomas' bride, the first homestead was erected, a smart 1860s edifice, with totora shingles on the roof. The little cottage became the schoolroom for the children and

ABOVE: The Natusch-designed Okawa homestead c 1900.   BELOW: The Okawa homestead as it stands today.

later the trophy room, adorned with silver cups won by animals bred on the station at various agriculture shows. Maria did much of the original tree planting, many of which remain today. Some of these were later cut out by TH, who said that while sheep were under the trees they were not eating grass or growing wool. Not only did he cut them down, but he placed a curb on more planting.

But TH could never contain Marsie's drive and enthusiasm. As she continued to make an enormous impact at Okawa, she brought in a brilliant early New Zealand architect, Charles Natusch – responsible for some of the most magnificent homes built in the early 20th century in the Wellington, Wairarapa, Hawke's Bay and Taranaki regions – to replace the original homestead. Natusch designed an impressive homestead, using part of the original. The ground floor was on three levels, with pumice being used as insulation between the panelling. Sadly, all the chimneys fell down in the 1931 Hawke's Bay earthquake. Other cottages were built at Okawa for the groom, gardeners and managers. Three built before 1900 are still lived in today.

This was the class into which Tom was born. He had a mother of immense substance, demonstrative, a driving, ambitious parent, kind-hearted, but demanding of the best for her children. And he had a father who was hard-working, mild-mannered and ambitious, but dedicated to the land and his sports pursuits. He was especially skilled in the finer points of cricket, golf and, later, horse-racing.

While they were among the elite of a more prosperous New Zealand as it entered a new century, what had enthused Ewart Grogan about the Lowrys and the Watt-Colemans was that their wealth had been won by hard graft and ingenuity. And Grogan recognised the New Zealand colonists as mainly from humble origins, and not "Johnnies", as he described his own countrymen.

These influences all helped shape the make-up of Tom as he entered an early life of privilege and almost unlimited opportunity.

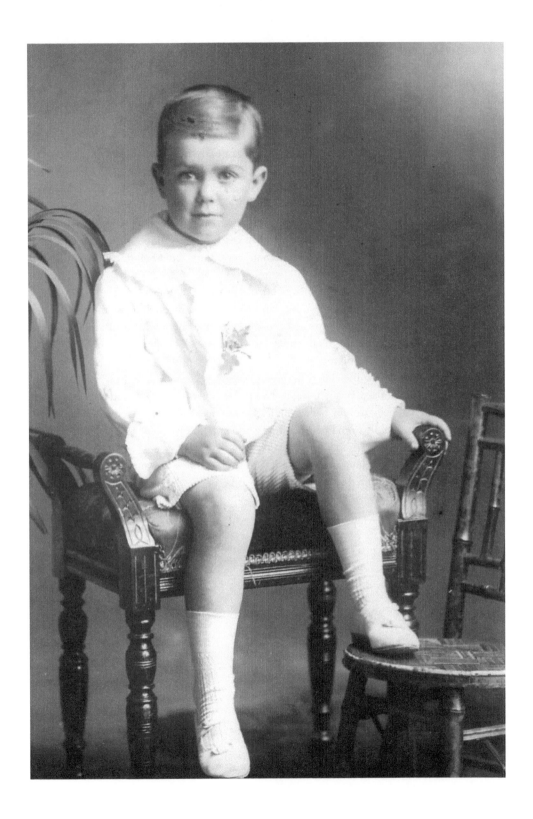

3. Growing Up

In a family used to sons and heirs, Tom's birth on February 2, 1898, must have been greeted with some relief, although TH and Marise needed to have little cause for concern – Tom was soon joined by brothers Jim and Ralph, as well as his sisters Gertrude (Beet) and Marion. Early photographs show Tom to be a bright-eyed, healthy, well-built youngster.

His pre-school formative years were blessed by an upbringing on a booming sheep station, rich with access to beef and mutton, a climate designed for the harvesting of superb fruit, berries and vegetables, lawns and fields on which to stretch growing legs, and an abundance of fresh air with hot, endless summers and not unduly harsh winters.

In the original Okawa Cottage, which became an on-site classroom, Tom began his schooling under the tutelage of a governess. He was then enrolled at Heretaunga Preparatory School in Hastings in 1908, a school that was merged with Hurworth from Wanganui in 1913, the year after Tom's departure to Christ's College. In 1927, it became Hereworth. Judging by Tom's academic record in his first year at Christ's, it's likely he paid due attention to his governess because by all accounts he excelled in the classroom at Heretaunga. The curriculum at Heretaunga was entirely traditional, with English, Latin, French, maths and divinity dominating the timetable.

Tom's headmaster when he arrived at Heretaunga was William Gray, a Cambridge graduate with an honours degree in mathematics. The school history describes him as "a rather cold and forbidding man... early photographs suggest a man who was brisk and energetic". One characteristic of his later years remained in the recollections of the old boys: "He suffered then from an undignified and uncomfortable complaint which led him to scratch the afflicted part when he felt the need for relief." Nevertheless, Gray gave great encouragement to sport and during his time arrangements were made to lease part of the school grounds to the Hastings Cricket Association.

This affinity with sport of the headmaster helped Tom, who began to build his cricket prowess. He assisted immeasurably by an English professional coach, Jack Board, who was engaged by the Hawke's Bay Cricket Association from 1909. In later years the Lowry boys were accused of being good cricketers only because their father brought out an English coach for their sole benefit, but this charge was far from the truth. Board was, in fact, the fourth professional engaged by Hawke's Bay, following in the footsteps of the original appointment, Albert Trott, an Australian who immigrated to England and played for Middlesex. This professional coaching era in Hawke's Bay was largely driven, not by TH Lowry, but by

LEFT: Tom before starting school, already showing signs of his future build and strength, but he wouldn't remain as angelic.

Heathcote Williams, at that time president of the association (and later the New Zealand Cricket Council), an unstinting servant of the game. Williams frequently used his own money to fund the coaching programme and also acted as guarantor for international touring teams to the Bay. TH played a part as a consistent contributor to the coaching initiative and there were others who gave generously as well.

So enthusiastic was Williams about the coaching programme that he went to England to find a new coach and, with the help of Lord Hawke, engaged Board, an appointment that was to last seven years. Board, who had been discovered by WG Grace – enabling him to graduate from gardener to professional cricketer – was an outstanding wicketkeeper who eventually became a prolific run-scorer for Gloucestershire and England.

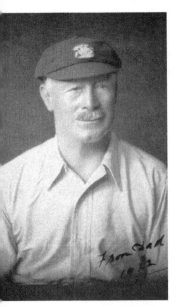

Hawke's Bay coach Jack Board, who exhorted Tom to "jump out and 'it 'em sir".

When Board arrived in Napier in early November, he was immediately thrust into work running a coaching session with the Napier High School boys. Frank Cane was one of the lucky players to receive his first instruction from Board: "Get your left foot across to the ball, sir." A schoolboy being addressed as "sir" rather tickled Cane, because it was certainly not the New Zealand way. Tom and the boys soon got used to another favourite Board exhortation: "Jump out and 'it 'em, sir." Board had come from coaching English public schools and knew his place.

Where TH's help for Tom and his brothers may have come into play was a requirement for Board to work with the cricket boys at Heretaunga. It seems Tom as an 11-year-old was being coached by Board even before the end of 1909, and the level of instruction increased with his place in the Heretaunga first X1 in 1910 and 1911. With TH still vitally interested in the game, and annual matches at Okawa on the Bay cricket programme, Board would have also visited the Grove, probably playing in select X1s and getting to know the Lowry family.

The year after Board's arrival, and with Tom just 12, the budding cricketer played for "Board's Colts" against a "Veterans X1" captained by a local Reverend, AP Clark. Going in at No 8 Tom, managed to cobble together one run for each of his 12 years and was left not out.

So captivated was Frank Cane with Board's work that years later in his excellent Hawke's Bay history, *Cricket Centenary*, he wrote: "Those who watched him in the nets could scarcely fail to notice with what vim and enthusiasm he entered into his work, and the very real pleasure he derived from his association with the boys. Here was a man indeed, not only gifted with the subtle art of imparting knowledge to the young, but who so gloried in it and so greatly enjoyed every moment of it, that he infused into the pupils themselves that very enthusiasm which is such an important requisite if the learner is to make good. The younger his charges the better Board liked it, and he greatly liked to set them on the right road from the start than to waste time eliminating faults which had already been acquired." This was the case for Tom. He was at the perfect age for soaking up Board's nurturing and the timing of the Heathcote Williams and TH Lowry philanthropy couldn't have worked out better.

A description of Tom's cricket abilities at this time appeared in the Heretaunga Prep school magazine of 1911, when he was an opening batsman and wicketkeeper in the first X1. "A promising but rather inconsistent bat. He has some great strokes on the off. Plays back far too much. Has shown great improvement as a wicketkeeper. Keeps well awake to a chance of stumping and has brought off some very fine pieces of work. At times has a tendency to snatch at the ball instead of getting in front of it."

Judging by Tom's progress over the next few years, it's likely Jack Board allowed him to follow his instinctive shot-making approach to batting. It wasn't until his county cricket days that he was forced to reassess and tighten up his defensive game.

With TH having attended Christ's College, it was almost inevitable that Tom's secondary schooling would be at the same school in Christchurch. Christ's College remains New Zealand's oldest secondary school and has long been the preferred place of learning for the sons of high income-earners. In Tom's day particularly it was a favoured school for the sons of North Island east coast run-holders. The boys' lengthy travel from North to South Island was helped by the regularity of shipping plying up and down the east coast. So each term the sons of the wealthy would be picked up in Tolaga Bay, Tokomaru Bay, Gisborne and Napier before heading to Lyttelton and Christchurch, avoiding the treacherous and much-feared Cook Strait.

In 1851 Bishop Selwyn had written in one Christchurch newspaper: "Mark out a good area of land and put up a wooden building. People are very tolerant and will call it 'The College'." While, as it developed, the College earned a well-deserved reputation for academic excellence, Christ's, established in a province that has always loved its sport, has also produced many who went on to win honours in national and international competition. The capacity to achieve at sport was helped by some forethought in the 1870s with the lease in perpetuity of playing fields in South Hagley Park, subsequently enlarged to 14 acres, which the college still has.

Tom arrived at Christ's in 1912. Placed in Moreland's House (which became School House), he was immediately ready for all aspects of college life. Besides his dominance as a sports figure, Tom also excelled as a scholar. In his first year at Christ's he finished the third term first in his class of 31 – first in Latin, winning the form prize; second in English and sixth in French. Where he didn't do so well was in maths (which he improved upon in subsequent years) and divinity, in which he was near the bottom of the class, despite his lineage from an English Reverend. Later when Tom became a school prefect, the headmaster, George Blanch, almost certainly had Tom in mind when he lectured the school prefects on reading the lesson in chapel, reminding them that the Bishop came to chapel every morning. Fellow prefect George Burdon remembered that on one occasion Tom read the lesson "particularly badly" and finished by saying: "Here endeth the wrong lesson."

Through 1913 his maths made a marked improvement, and he moved to third in his class by the end of the year, with an overall placing of sixth out of 22. Through his college years he continued to concentrate on French, Latin and English, as well as being part of a small group studying Greek. In his fourth year he won the set prize for Greek. In 1916, his last year, he won the mid-year prizes for Latin and English, as well as passing matriculation, solicitors general knowledge and medical preliminary. However, the Christ's training route to law and medicine was never to feature on Tom's horizon.

In Don Hamilton's *College! A History of Christ's College,* Tom is described as an "outstanding figure of the war years". He may have done well academically, but the strength of his personality and his powerful physique gave him dominance in the sports arena that few could equal. By his second year he was in the shooting VIII, had progressed to the 1st X1, becoming captain in his last two years, 1915 and 1916. In the same two years he played for the 1st XV, captaining the team in 1916. This year was a busy one, because not only was Tom captaining the cricket and rugby teams, but he was also captain of cadets and a prefect. He still had time to win the heavyweight boxing title by knocking out George Gerard, a future Bishop of Waiapu, in the final. As head of house (boarding), he earned a reputation for helping to overcome the feeble discipline of headmaster Blanch, where canings were still being administered by prefects, although in this year the prefects were told to stop "throwing in" at the baths. Later (after Tom had departed) Blanch also pulled the prefects up for smoking in the intervals at dances, saying that not only did it harm the name of the school, but was also "very bad for the individual cases where the boys had not reached the age of 19".

This sort of directive would have flown over Tom's head. He almost certainly started smoking in his college days and remained an inveterate smoker for the rest of his life.

Like Jack Board's presence and influence in Tom's days at Heretaunga, there were more cricket brains to assist his progress at Christ's. The first X1 coach during his early years at the school was Jimmy Lawrence, a former New Zealand representative. Lawrence, who had also played for Canterbury, had a reputation for cautious batting, but it's unlikely this would have unduly influenced Tom's natural bent for aggressive strokeplay. More to his liking may have been another former New Zealand player, Harold Lusk, who happened to be Tom's form teacher in 1916. Lusk at this time was still playing for Canterbury, a batsman capable of spectacular hitting, confident and strong on the on-side and described by MCC player PR May in 1906-07 as "looking to be the best bat in the colony". Lawrence and Lusk were sometimes pitted against Tom in teams that met the first X1.

Another influence was Canterbury and New Zealand left-arm medium-pace bowler Tom Carlton, who the college engaged to bowl to the boys in the nets. In 1912, his first year at the college, Tom came up against all three coaches in his one appearance that year for the first X1. The team, skippered by Lawrence, also included a New Zealand keeper, Charles Boxshall.

Most of Tom's cricket in his first year was played for the third X1, and his promotion for the one first X1 appearance may have been because of a brilliant 150 not out for the Boarders against the Boys.

By 1913 his position in the first X1 was secure, despite the fact that he never really got going with the bat. His second year in the team, however, was much more productive, although *The Register* for December 1914 alluded to impetuosity with his batting that often led to his downfall. "Lowry, as well as being a wicketkeeper of considerable merit, is quite the finest bat in the team, and can score well all round the wicket; he should have made more runs, but has yet to learn that he must play himself in before taking liberties with the bowling." Against Linwood, he scored 91 not out in a total of 129, and he followed up with 126 against North Town.

The years 1915-20 have been described as the golden years of cricket at Christ's. Three captains in this era, Tom Lowry, Roger Blunt and Ron Talbot, went on to play for New

Captain of Christ's College first X1, 1916.

Zealand, with Blunt touring England under Tom's captaincy in 1927 and 1931 and Talbot on the 1931 tour. The old inconsistency with the bat, though, was still blighting Tom's performances in 1915. *The Register* noted: "Lowry, who is as good a wicketkeeper as ever, has up to the present failed to do himself full justice, but he is bound to get runs before the season is over. He can score with ease all round the wicket, but often falls victim to a ball that deserves no better fate than to be despatched to the boundary for four." The skipper earned praise for the amount of time he put in to improve the standard of the team's fielding.

During these first X1 days, Tom was capable of performing in all aspects of the game (as he did for most of his career) and was just as likely to bowl as to keep wicket. In 1916, in the traditional fixture against Otago Boys' High, played at Carisbrook, Christ's scored 300 in the first innings before rain intervened and then Tom took advantage of a rain-damaged wicket to take 5-7 off seven overs as Otago were dismissed for 114, before falling to an innings defeat.

The college at this time was also playing in the Christchurch senior club competition (depleted by players serving in the war) and this enabled leading players like Tom and Roger Blunt to sharpen their skills against mature and experienced players in a much more competitive environment. In his final year at Christ's, Tom was joined in the first X1 by his brother, Jim, who, after Tom left, played for two years under Roger Blunt. The youngest Lowry brother, Ralph, made the X1 in 1919.

For a schoolboy, Tom could be an explosive batsman. Against Christchurch Boys' High School, when Roger Blunt was still a skinny youngster, they came together needing 60 runs

Tom, second row, far right, ready for action with a heavily-bandaged right knee. Christ's College, first XV, 1915.

to win. Half an hour later the game was over, Blunt having secured two singles and Tom the other 58. Tom was assisted by the opposing captain putting on a young Curly Page, bowling gentle off-breaks. Tom promptly lofted five of these over the Hagley Park hedge at mid-wicket. On another occasion against Christchurch Boys', he came in at first drop and hit 27 off the first two overs he faced.

It was clear that Tom's sports future, if there was to be one, would revolve around cricket. Rugby certainly interested him, and he played effectively as both a back and forward during his Christ's days, but he never gained the traction apparent in the summer game. He was a forward in the 1912 fifth XV, but by his first year in the first XV, three years later, he was playing in the three-quarters. In one match, won 69-0 by Christ's, he touched down for five tries. He was badly affected by injuries this year, reducing his appearances. The following year, as captain, he returned to the forwards.

As the eldest son of TH and Marsie, there was an expectation that Tom would eventually take over the running of Okawa. It is also likely that TH planned that the boys would all finish their education at Cambridge University, following in his own footsteps and those of his father. That posed difficulties in 1917 because of the war, and Tom returned to Okawa as a sheep station cadet. While the boys had been brought up on the land, developing a hands-on expertise in many aspects of farm life now became more important. Knowledge of animal husbandry, quality pasture maintenance, wool clips and shepherding became part of Tom's life as he took on the role of farmer.

It was also time for Tom and his brothers, now young men, to loosen the shackles of home life and they took it upon themselves to bypass the old Fernhill Hotel "out of bounds" rule.

For this they enlisted the services of Lofty, the draught horse who, as the night darkened, would pull TH's Cadillac noiselessly across the paddock past the homestead. The exercise would be repeated on their return in the early hours of the morning. According to Ralph, the housemaids and parlour maids were also out of bounds but "they were better looking than the girls in Hastings", so they would go along as well.

Yet, as much as he loved life on the land, Tom, seeing no end in sight for the war, developed a strong desire to play a part. He enlisted, but then made the decision to transfer from the army to the air force, which almost certainly, because of delays, cost him the chance of active war service. Why he chose flying remains a mystery, but the glamour, lure of adventure and youthful exuberance would all have played a part in Tom's decision. With flying still in its infancy, he was entering the most hazardous vocation in the war effort.

Ian Mackersey in *Smithy: The Life of Sir Charles Kingsford Smith,* described how in 1916 the Flying Corp aeroplanes were primitive and downright dangerous to fly, and life expectancy was measured in weeks. "Death and injury was a statistical inevitability...with the pilot's worst fear, the daily prospect of being burned...The art of flying training hardly existed while many of the trainers were psychologically damaged from their own flying...the noise of the planes was deafening, the cold intense. Directions were shouted above the roar of the engines and the cockpits were open to the elements."

For budding New Zealand pilots, practical training during the war years was done by private enterprise in two flying schools – the New Zealand Flying School at Kohimarama on the Auckland Harbour and the Canterbury Aviation Company at Sockburn. Auckland's school owed its existence to two motor engineers, Leo and Vivian Walsh, who had been experimenting with the building of aeroplanes since 1910.

The Walsh brothers started by trying to build a land plane but, after some unhappy experiences, decided to try their hands at a flying boat. This was still under construction when the war broke out and was eventually launched at Bastion Point on New Year's Day, 1915. After a number of successful trials, they considered it suitable for training pilots. While the Government was prepared to offer only moral support, a signal was sent to the British Government, asking whether New Zealand-trained pilots would be acceptable to the Royal Flying Corp and what qualifications they would require. Back came the reply that all suitable candidates qualifying for the Royal Aero Club's certificate in New Zealand would be accepted for commissions in the Royal Flying Corps.

Based on the private enterprise aspect of this venture, it naturally helped if the ambitious flyers had the means to pay for their course. Tom, of course, did, but to overcome the pain of the £100 payment ($10,000 in today's terms), which covered learning to fly plus an engineering course, there was an incentive of a £75 refund when each successful candidate arrived in England, and first-class fares were to be paid as well.

Despite these pay-as-you-go requirements, applications for training were so numerous that the Walsh brothers formed a limited liability company to finance the purchase of two more aircraft. In addition, they built another aircraft themselves, so that by 1916 they had a fleet of four. Three pilots were trained in 1915. Later courses increased to 12 and, by the time of Tom's entry in 1917-18, to 25, with this output occurring every six months. Tom received his certificate after flying a Curtiss flying boat in April 1918. As required for all qualifying flights,

Tom's effort was witnessed by military officers appointed by the New Zealand Government. By the end of the war, 110 pupils had been trained by the school and Tom was one of the 68 to receive commissions in the Royal Flying Corps or Royal Air Force. Eight were to receive the Distinguished Flying Cross.

An indication of how Tom was viewed at this time, particularly by the opposite sex, came in a letter to Margot later in life. "I doted on Tom when he was at the flying school at Auckland, as did all females who met him (I had no views to matrimony), but he was lucky to escape and lucky enough to fall in love with you."

Training to fly, perhaps interspersed by some flirtatious interludes, was never enough for someone as energetic and versatile as Tom. When he arrived in Auckland towards the end of 1917, he joined the University Cricket Club and by round two of the senior competition was in action against the Eden club. For much of his season he opened the batting for the club and he was immediately successful, scoring 62 in his first innings. Early in the New Year he notched 70 against Grafton and top-scored with 16 in a dismal total of 49 against Parnell, as well as taking 3-29 in the same match. These efforts were enough to impress the Auckland selectors, who picked him for the match against Wellington, starting on January 26. This became his first-class debut.

Handsome, debonair Tom at his flying graduation. He was doted on by women.

Surprisingly, he played as the side's wicketkeeper. In his club side, the keeping duties were looked after by Wilson Garrard, later an Auckland and New Zealand player, and Tom's keeping selection was clearly on reputation. Auckland's incumbent keeper was brilliant stumper Dick Rowntree, a fixture in the team from 1914 until after the war, but he wasn't available in the early part of 1918.

It was a satisfactory debut for Tom, who batted at No 9. Auckland were well beaten by an innings, but in the first innings Tom batted with Syd Smith, the former West Indian and English county player, the pair adding 63 for the eighth wicket before Tom was bowled by Stan Brice for 28. Brice also bowled him in the second innings, but he was able to add a stumping and two catches to his debut effort in Wellington's only innings. Included in the Wellington team was his old Christ's College form teacher Harold Lusk, who at the time was in camp at Trentham and was given dispensation to turn out for Wellington.

Back in club cricket and based on his wicketkeeping efforts for Auckland, he was handed the gloves and secured two stumpings in his next outing. It proved to be a very solid club season for Tom, with another two half-centuries, and he finished with 447 runs and averaged 30.

There was time for one more first-class appearance, the return match against Wellington at the Basin Reserve. Wellington were again dominant, winning by an innings. Tom, batting at No 8, fell cheaply in both innings, for 9 and 1.

With the cricket season over, Tom flew for his aero training certificate. This he passed on April 22, 1918, and by the following month he was sailing to Britain with the 37th reinforcements. His active service began on May 9, and the following February, after further training, he was commissioned as 2nd Lieutenant, joining the Royal Air Force. But the war had ended in November, so he saw no active service. In June 1919, he was demobilised after 282 of days of service.

(Hydro-aeroplane)   6016

LOWRY, Thomas Coleman
      Okawa, Hastings, Hawkes Bay, New Zealand

Born 17th Feb., 1898   at Hastings, New Zealand
Nationality   British
Rank, Regiment, Profession   Sheep Station Cadet
Certificate taken on   Curtiss Flying Boat
At New Zealand Flying School, Kohimarama, Auck-
                                        land.
Date 22nd April, 1918.

From the records of the Royal Air Force.

4. The Roaring Twenties

By 1919, the allies were basking in the afterglow of victory in World War I. The conflict, a war to end all wars, or so it was said at the time, had not only governments but the masses demanding "never again" and "no more" – increasingly popular slogans at the start of the next decade.

While Tom had not seen action, his air force service had put him alongside many young men turned old by the horrors of war. This widespread evidence of suffering and abhorrence of war produced a natural societal reaction – bury the past and loosen up a bit. The Roaring Twenties, as they became known, did just that. The decade ushered in nightclubs serving cocktails, the jazz era was launched, spawning gramophones and the first crystal radios, women, aspiring to be slender and flat-chested, with the faces of 15-year-olds, smoked cigarettes in public and attended fitness clubs. They also wore cloche hats while the men paraded in knickerbockers and two-tone shoes. The Flapper era had arrived. It was martini time and Tom, in his prime, was a willing participant.

While there was fun to be had, there seemed little reason for an early return to New Zealand. More importantly, TH and Marsie were now considering the future advancement of their young adult family, and this could be best achieved by the boys' attendance at Cambridge University and the girls' at a finishing school. This meant a shift for the entire family to England (with managers in place at Okawa), although it wasn't without resistance from TH. Normally mild-mannered and gentlemanly, he balked so badly at these sojourns to England that he was heard to remark that he would rather spend the winter in the Napier jail. TH hated leaving Okawa and his horses, and he particularly disliked the old family home at Carlisle. Because of this, Marsie bought a house from the Hudsons, who were relatives of the Lowrys in Cumberland, at which point TH said: "I'll come, but I'm not paying a penny." This was a much larger house than the old family home and could accommodate more guests and friends, so provided the opportunity for entertaining.

With the war over, Tom had plenty of time to indulge his sports pursuits and much of his cricket in 1919 was for Air Force and Combined Services teams. There was an appearance for Leveson Gower's X1 against Oxford University, Tom's third first-class match. Tom didn't exactly mark the occasion as he would have wanted, recording a pair of spectacles in a game washed out after two days.

About this time Tom may have also gone to Africa or India for a spot of big-game hunting, but this remains only anecdotal. Tom Junior questioned him on this in later life but, as with his memories of the war (where he grieved the loss of so many cricket friends), he was reluctant to expand, "probably thinking I would get the wrong idea". Tom was an excellent shot, his prowess enhanced by an enormous amount of practice in the fleet air arm. Pilots were required to shoot at the enemy out of their windows and this was fine-tuned by shooting clay birds. His love of grouse shooting in England had probably also revealed itself by this time.

While Tom was still undecided about university, it seems the influence of his brothers convinced him Cambridge was the place to be and by the start of the 1920 university year (August) he had arrived.

University for Tom was never going to lead to a life in the "City". Peter Roebuck in *From Sammy to Jimmy* describes how Tom played for Somerset while studying at Cambridge. "Not that studying is sufficiently broad a word to capture Lowry's range of activities, for he was a tough, gregarious, adventurous fellow. At university he was member of the Hellfire Club, to qualify for which a man had to blow three smoke rings and spit through them. He was not inclined to take his degree too seriously, and was apt to wander off to the Newmarket races, once departing with a £5 note and returning with a small motor car. A drinking man, he disdained anaesthetic at the dentist and once, in his cups, referred to someone important at Lord's as 'an old faggot' – a remark happily forgotten by the time Lowry returned as captain of his country."

A few years later Tom, back in New Zealand, decided, while having a tooth extracted, that the dentist's anaesthetic might now be a good idea. The dentist gave him the needle to deaden the pain and then got to work on the molar. After five minutes Tom exclaimed: "Don't you think I ought to send for the blacksmith!" Back came the dentist's reply: "Don't be a bloody fool, Tom. I'm not trying to pull the tooth; I'm merely rocking its foundations."

Cambridge days. Tom, fourth from right, back row.

At Cambridge, the place where one was least likely to find Tom was in his rooms. He was eventually elected president of the Hawks club (a collection of Blues and semi-Blues), where he dispensed New Zealand informality and friendliness to all, plus, in equal measure, unsolicited racing advice. Many of his tips were right because of his instinctive accuracy on how a horse would run, and some said he was much prouder of this accomplishment than his ability to read how a ball was going to turn. In his early days at Cambridge, he also played fullback for Jesus College rugby team. Here his method was that of an immovable rock – he would allow himself to be run into, causing so many casualties that for the good name of the college he had to give up his winter amusement. A Cambridge friend said: "This was regrettable, because large crowds used to turn up at otherwise uninteresting college matches in order to see famous three-quarters bouncing off Tom."

Tom's method of scraping through the exams at Cambridge was to employ a cramming tutor in the third term. When he related this to his daughter Carol, he made no explanation as to what he was up to in terms one and two. All the boys left Cambridge with degrees – Tom a BA in history; Jim an MA in law and geography; and Ralph a BA in law and political economy before going on to complete his MA after the war.

None of the boys used their degrees in their careers, because they were born to the land. But academically they were very capable and the combination of a university qualification and their immersion in the university of life served them admirably in their future travails. It was said that when the boys arrived at Cambridge they were instructed by TH and Marsie to not return until they had obtained their Blues and all three did, Jim in tennis, Ralph in rugby and, of course, Tom in cricket.

By 1920, when he went to Cambridge, Tom was starting to be noticed as a cricketer and at the completion of the university season he was included in an Incogniti Cricket Club team that toured America and Canada. The invitation may well have arisen because of Incogniti's close association with the services. There were a number of luminaries in the team, the foremost being Douglas Jardine, then at Oxford, plus a former England player, Major Teddy Wynyard, and various county players. This quality appeared incompatible with the likely opposition and it was no surprise that the Incogniti were unbeaten in their nine matches.

The major matches were against the Philadelphia Cricket Club, when the *New York Herald* noted (in a report by "Spartan Cricketer") that Jardine "had hardly gotten set when he was caught at the wicket for a duck egg". Later the *New York Times* changed its tune when, against a New York X1, "the sensation of the first day's play was the wonderful stand of 157 made by PR Jardini [sic]. In compiling this total, the Briton made 7 boundaries and a six, the later hit being a smash over the fence on the locker end of the field." Individual details of the tour are sketchy, with only century-makers recorded, and there is no record of Tom's efforts. Nevertheless, he must have impressed skipper Evelyn Metcalfe, because when Incogniti returned to the United States under his leadership in 1924, Tom was again part of the team.

Tom played a much more prominent role second time round, finishing second in the batting averages. He scored a century against the Merion Cricket Club and 56 not out against Frankford, when he shared a big partnership with Arthur Gilligan. He captained the side in both these matches and Incogniti were unbeaten again in their seven games. Tom was in his element on these tours. He could indulge his passion for cricket, he loved the comradeship of

The Incogniti team that toured the United States in 1924. Back row: Guy Earl, Tom, Trevor Arnott, Joe Thorley, Geoffrey Cuthbertson, Jim White, Arthur Gilligan, Philip Irwin. Front row: Thomas Brocklebank, Evelyn Metcalfe (captain), Harry Hargreaves, George Hickson, Tom Landale.

like-minded amateurs and enjoyed the often lavish hospitality.

An indication of what these tours were like off the field came after the 1920 American sojourn, when the Philadelphian Pilgrims paid a return visit to England in 1921. The players expressed delight with their welcome, their only complaint being that the lavish hospitality extended to them was hardly conducive to good cricket.

There were some colleagues Tom wasn't so keen on, and he openly showed disdain for superior young Englishmen. On the trip to America, one of the team, an unpopular young Old Etonian, booked a whole suite on the top deck while four of the six-footers, including Tom, shared a cabin in the bowels of the ship. In Tom's first match as captain, as he led the team on to the field, the player sidled up to Tom and loftily observed: "Lowry, I usually field in the slips," to which Tom replied: "Well, you'll have a bloody good chance on this tour to practise fielding somewhere else."

By 1921, now resident at Cambridge, Tom's aim was to win his Blue for the university. At the beginning of May, with spring still in the air, he hammered 183 in the Freshman match, but still couldn't make the side. Historians record this 1921 team as the best Cambridge team of the 20th century. It included the three outstanding Ashton brothers, with Gilbert, the eldest, (nicknamed Ashton Villa) the captain, England players Percy Chapman, Jack MacBryan, "Father" Marriott, Jack Bryan, and other quality players like Dar Lyon (regarded as one of the best cricketers never to play for England) and Clem Gibson. *Wisden* recorded that "Lowry would have easily gained his Blue in an ordinary year" and "it is impossible to see who could have been left out of the side".

There may have been one other reason for Tom's non-selection. There was a natural antipathy between Tom and the Ashtons. Tom was known to take offence at what he considered the affected speech and superior airs of many English under-graduates of the time and he thought the Ashtons unduly straight-laced. His reaction was to portray a rough, hard-swearing, hard-drinking colonial. In one early appearance for the university, he had his pads on about half an hour before the close of play, ready to bat as the next man in. Lined up in the bar were two un-drunk whiskies, when the Cambridge skipper came in and

Tom at the time of his Somerset county career.

said: "Tom, if another wicket falls and you have to go in tonight I don't want you to take any risks." Five minutes later, a wicket fell. Tom downed the two whiskies and strode to the wicket. Ignoring the instructions, he rattled up 20 runs in short time and next day went on to complete a half-century. That was his last appearance for Cambridge that season.

Nevertheless, a lack of cricket for Cambridge resulted in significant benefits for his future. The first was qualification to play for Somerset. About this time, Somerset captain John Daniell, known as "The Prophet", started a recruiting campaign, targeting in particular Cambridge and Oxford Universities. He didn't pay over-much attention to qualification rules. The first and abiding requirement of these rules was birth in the county concerned, and a rule that any player shifting to a new county would need to live there for two years before qualifying. There was considerable attention on this issue in the early 1920s, particularly concerning Walter Hammond and his eligibility for Gloucestershire. While Hammond was the most notable of the offenders, there were others and the four or five in question were pursued with some vigour by train-spotting administrators. All of this was presided over by Lord Harris, then known as the "King of Cricket" and the chief eagle-beagle at Lord's. Harris was an autocratic leader who had an influence in just about every major English cricket decision for 50 years.

Tom's qualification for Somerset is the story of legends. Terry McLean told it this way in *Silver Fern – 150 Years of New Zealand Sport*: "'Birthplace?' snapped Lord Harris, the all-powerful nabob at Lord's, when Lowry fronted. 'Wellington, sir,' said Lowry. 'Excellent,' said His Lordship. 'That charming spot in Somerset.'" While the story in this form is unlikely to have been true, what is fact is that Somerset, as a deliberate ploy, had been carrying on a charade when it came to player qualifications.

Tom was not the first New Zealander to use the Wellington ruse at Somerset. Peter Randall Johnson was educated at Eton and Cambridge and then back-doored into the county team in 1902 after Lord's asked where he had been born. Somerset's reply was Wellington, but no mention of New Zealand was made. The first New Zealander at Somerset, Johnson had little in common with Tom, except for his education path. Never popular (but respected

John Daniell, the Somerset captain who was such a strong influence on Tom.

for his batting) at Somerset, Johnson was not a mixer, much preferring "a game of poker on a Saturday night and a Dickens novel on a Sunday afternoon". He was always a picture of sartorial elegance, batting in Zingari colours and with a silk handkerchief knotted around his neck. He was known to stride into the pavilion, dressed to the nines, saying he had been doing a spot of work. By the time of Tom's arrival (with Johnson still playing occasional games), Somerset had no qualms in using the Wellington subterfuge again, no doubt backing the fact that if it worked once it would be a fait accompli the second time.

The second benefit from Tom's move to Somerset was the influence of the captain, John Daniell. Not only did Daniell put him up at his home in Taunton, but as Tom matured as a cricketer, many of his playing characteristics could be traced to the philosophy of his Somerset captain. Peter Roebuck said this of Daniell in his absorbing history of Somerset: "A fair cricketer, a combative captain, an outstanding leader, and a man with the courage of two lions, he was, perhaps, as impressive a man as has ever taken an active part in the directing of Somerset cricket affairs. Picture him, if you will, fielding in his Homburg, cursing a negligent cover-point, glaring at a timid batsman, and waiting upon the arrival between overs (and carried by a telegraph boy) of news of a horse upon whose fortunes he had placed his shirt. Picture him, afterwards, chatting with Len Braund, a fellow enthusiast, and promising a scotch or two upon stumps being drawn."

There were other aspects, too, that would have appealed to Tom. Daniell had captained England at rugby in the early 1900s, and later became president of the (England) Rugby Union. He was not interested in money (but, like Tom, had private means). Roebuck went on to say: "He entered the old Somerset idea of having a go, of playing with pride and character no matter the odds...he was charismatic, impetuous and decisive."

Some of these personal traits of Daniell were already part of Tom's persona – the courage and natural leadership, the socialising, the betting on the horses, the interest in rugby. And the captaincy lessons learned from Daniell were later filtered into Tom's leadership. His development in the practice of providing "commentary" (a 1920s version of sledging) on the run of play, the decisiveness and the unorthodox moves all owed something to what he absorbed at the knee of Daniell. And the rebel individualism in the wearing of his Moawhango club cap or the battered Homburg had overtones of a bit of his fellow New Zealander, Johnson, in the first instance, and Daniell in the second.

Through 1921 and 1922, Tom's efforts for Somerset were not spectacular, but showed enough to indicate that he was a player not only capable of performing well at county level, but one who could go further. *Wisden* said: "Great promise was shown by TC Lowry, who could not get his Blue at Cambridge, but was quite good enough for Somerset. He always did quite well and although his highest score was 56, he had an average of 26."

His Somerset team-mate, writer Raymond Robertson-Glasgow, had detected his age-old problem – sound defence – but Tom was working on it: "On to the build and inclination of a hitter, he grafted the technique and discipline of defence. You could, as it were, see the join; and there was nothing about it all that was beautiful to watch; but it could be fine to hear, when the boom of the sightscreen answered the crack of the bat."

Although he played more cricket in 1922, Tom's average was about the same as the previous year – 572 runs at 24.86 with a highest score of 77. After some barren years Somerset were an improving side, owing largely to Daniell's recruitment drive. Tom was part of a strong amateur batting line-up that included Dar Lyon, Jack MacBryan, Peter Johnson, John Daniell and Guy Earle. Robertson-Glasgow also wrote of his wicketkeeping at this time: "As a wicketkeeper Tom was tough, occasionally negligent, and often brilliant. He would start, perhaps, clumsily and miss some obvious chance, then he would wipe that out with some wonderful stumping off an in-swinger on the blind spot just outside the leg stump."

His wicketkeeping may have helped him make his next touring team, the Archie MacLaren-led 1922-23 MCC tour to New Zealand. Tom's selection was rather a quaint choice, given that he was a New Zealander, but his eligibility was based on his county and particularly university appearances (the side had a strong Oxbridge colour to it), and at that stage he had made no signal that he would be returning permanently to New Zealand.

The team was also something of a hotchpotch, given another MCC team touring South Africa at the same time had first priority on players. The best known of MacLaren's players were Percy Chapman, fast emerging as the golden-boy of English cricket and Tich Freeman, a quality leg-break and googly bowler. Both could count themselves very unlucky not to be touring South Africa.

The choice of MacLaren as captain almost beggars belief. At 51 years of age, he was a somewhat glorious relic of the past, a former captain of England and still holder, at this time, of the world first-class record, 424 for Lancashire against Somerset. Famous writer Neville Cardus, totally infatuated with the heroes of Lancashire, had written of MacLaren that "he didn't merely hook the ball, he dismissed it from his presence". MacLaren had another side to him that wasn't so attractive. He had a haughty air with a habit of rubbing people up the wrong way. In addition, he had a reputation for a lack of scruples in financial matters. So New Zealand was about to see a decidedly interesting character in action.

Bill Ferguson, the scorer on the tour, related one story that occurred in Melbourne before the MCC left for the New Zealand segment of their trip. Ferguson happened to be close by MacLaren as he was paying the hotel bill.

RIGHT: Raymond Robertson-Glasgow, a good cricketer and a great writer.

The 1922-23 MCC team to New Zealand. Back row: John McLean, Tich Freeman, Percy Chapman, Alex Wilkinson, Geoffrey Wilson, Harry Tyldesley, Charles Titchmarsh, Willie Hill-Wood, Bill Ferguson (scorer), David Brand, Freddie Calthorpe. Front row: Henry Swan, Archie MacLaren (captain), Viscount Jellicoe (New Zealand Governor-General), Jock Hartley, Tom, Clem Gibson.

Archie MacLaren, the aristocratic Lancastrian who captained the MCC team to New Zealand in 1922-23.

Programme from the unofficial test at the Basin Reserve, in which Archie MacLaren hit a double-century.

How a New Zealand caricaturist greeted the MCC team.

MacLaren said: "Lend me some cash. I haven't got enough to pay the champagne account." Ferguson handed over the required amount and wrote later: "MacLaren, with his expensive tastes, never even made a token attempt to make the tour pay its way, being first and foremost concerned with his own requirements."

MacLaren batted only nine times on tour before suffering injury. Nevertheless he showed he could still play by scoring 200 in the first unofficial test against New Zealand, at Wellington. Tom made a good 54 in a sixth-wicket stand with his skipper of 127 in just 63 minutes. MCC reached 505 and won by an innings.

Tom's 54 was the start of a very good effort in the internationals – 61 in the next at Christchurch, and then 130 in the third back at Wellington. The press reported after his century that "he got a great ovation as he returned to the pavilion, several of the crowd rushing to meet him and cheering lustily. Among those in the stand who applauded more quietly was a pleasant-faced lady, the lad's mother, who had keenly watched the match from its commencement. It was the first time she had seen her son score a century."

The local correspondent of the *Sydney Referee* described his style: "Most of the runs in his century were made with shots on the on-side, 50 of them in a semi-circle from square-leg to the bowler. The rising ball on the off he punches through the slips with a lot of pace."

The team was unbeaten in New Zealand, but in matches in Australia against strong state sides lost three times. Not everyone in New Zealand was happy with the tourists. The tour made a financial loss, and the tourists were described by some as aloof. In other quarters there was outrage that the two professionals in the side, Freeman and Tyldesley, were treated like servants and were made to sleep in separate hotels from the rest of the team. Tom had a mixed tour with the bat (654 runs at 27.25), but delivered in the "tests", and proved a capable back-up to the No 1 keeper, John McLean.

If 1921 and 1922 were his establishment seasons on the English cricket scene, Tom really benefited from what he had learnt during his time in MacLaren's team. In 1923 he showed far greater consistency and a presence in captaincy that helped forge his reputation in England. The catalyst to his improved fortunes was a scintillating 161 for Cambridge against Lancashire in the early part of the season. The innings, which included 17 fours and took just 170 minutes, secured his permanent place in the university side. Cambridge had a mediocre season, but Tom was clearly the superior batsman, scoring four centuries and averaging 49.

Unfortunately, the Cambridge v Oxford encounter at Lord's was a disaster for Cambridge. Oxford scored 422 and then bowled out Cambridge twice after a thunderstorm had ruined the pitch. Tom failed twice, but so did most of his team-mates, with the side scoring just 59 in the first innings and 136 in the second. Tom's future brother-in-law, Reg Bettington, had a field day with his leg-spinners and returned match figures of 11-87, including Tom's wicket in the second innings.

In this match, Tom was also up against his Somerset team-mate Robertson-Glasgow. "Cruso", as he was known, claimed he was such an inferior batsman that he seldom troubled to own a bat. He usually borrowed one from a batsman friend who didn't mind, based on the fact that Crusoe was unlikely to stay in long enough to damage it. As Robertson-Glasgow was shaping up to face a ball from one of the Cambridge bowlers, Tom chipped in from short leg: "Do you buy a new bat every match Robbie, or keep it in the bath overnight?" There was temporary hold-up while the batsman and the keeper recovered their composure.

There was still time for a number of appearances for Somerset and his total first-class runs for the season was 1564 at an average of 35.54. *Wisden* said: "When getting a big score he was one of the most brilliant hitters of the year."

By 1924, Tom had become the subject of behind-the-scenes manoeuvring that had the potential for unpleasantness. The Cambridge captain-designate for 1924 was Gubby Allen, later an England captain, MCC chairman and pillar of the MCC establishment. Tradition had it that the Blues met after the university match to elect their captain for the following season. Overshadowing Allen's appointment was the fact that he was going to be sent down from Trinity College through a lack of study, although an appointment as captain would have resulted in another college happily picking him up as an undergraduate. Then shock. At the meeting, the current captain, Claude Ashton, nominated as his successor, not Gubby (who as captain-designate was not present), but the "colonial Tom Lowry". Tom was duly elected. Jim Swanton takes up the story in *Gubby Allen – Man of Cricket:* "When Ashton and Gubby had talked the matter over beforehand, Gubby had said words to the effect that if Ashton felt he wanted to put up someone else as captain he would not take it amiss. At the meeting, however, according to Leonard Crawley, who was present, Ashton said, 'Gubby would be quite happy not to be appointed' – a very distinct difference of emphasis. Leonard, incidentally favoured a free vote in camera rather than in cold blood round the table, since no-one likes to vote against a friend in public, even though he may not consider him a suitable candidate."

According to Swanton, Allen harboured no hard feelings on being passed over, but made the pointed comment that "the Ashtons had never appreciated Lowry", whereas, he said, he had made it a first priority as secretary to make him [Tom] welcome in the side and persona grata with the captain.

Many years later HEB Newton (Newt), a Wanganui cricketer and a cricket historian who knew Tom well (and had a fund of stories on Lowry, the best of which he ruefully confided, were unprintable), confirmed on good authority that the Ashtons couldn't stand Lowry. Swanton's reference to "the colonial Lowry" would have been an accurate description of how Claude Ashton saw the class distinction between his family and someone from the antipodes (although Gubby Allen was born in Australia

Tom, the first New Zealand cricketer to appear on a cigarette card.

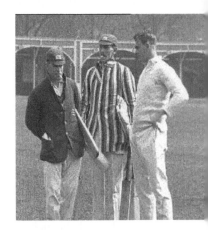

Tom (right), captain of Cambridge, conferring with England batting great Patsy Hendren (left).

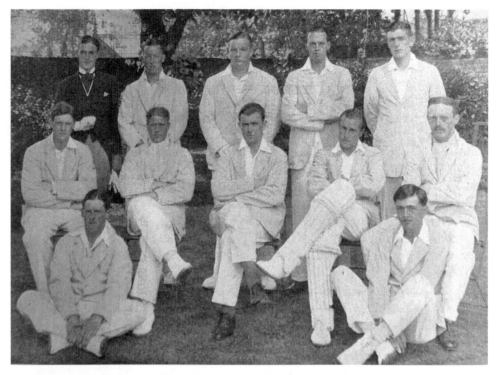

The 1924 Cambridge team. Back row: Cecil Bennett, Jim White, Harold Austin, William Shirley, Jack Meyer. Middle row: Noel Sherwell, Philip Wright, Tom (captain), Henry Enthoven, Leonard Crawley. Front row: James Mann, Eddie Dawson.

before moving, as a six-year-old, to England). Ashton would have been even less impressed when after his appointment, in 1924, Tom led Cambridge on to the field at Lord's in his battered Homburg, and it most certainly did not please the Long Room habitués. The Ashtons may also have heard the story of Tom's reference of a Lord's identity being "an old faggot".

So why did Claude Ashton nominate Tom instead of Gubby Allen? There appears to be two options. The first was that he wanted Allen even less than Lowry. The second may have been based on age. Allen would have been 20 coming up 21 on assuming the captaincy whereas by 1924 Tom would be 26, and more ready for the responsibility of the role. While Tom won the job, both were excellent candidates and capable of taking on the responsibility. Both went on to captain their respective countries.

There was no glorious march to the mantle of captaincy for Tom. First he was struck down by appendicitis at the start of the season, which meant when he eventually came back he was less than his robust, bustling self. His demeanour was further darkened by severe teeth problems.

The side he took over was much changed from the previous season and the 1923 team, despite its heavy loss in the university match, was recognised as a superior combination. Gone were the likes of Claude Ashton and Ronnie Aird, and there were few of similar quality to replace them. Nevertheless Tom took to the leadership with gusto, introducing a policy of

Two New Zealand sports powerhouses of the 1920s – Tom and All Black captain Maurice Brownlie.

fitness and concentration on fielding to make up for some of the weaknesses in other aspects of the game, such as inconsistent batting.

When Cambridge got to the university match at Lord's in July, they had sustained a number of losses, including a thumping by the touring South Africans. But the mediocre performances were all turned round against Oxford, with Tom leading from the front. Oxford were bowled out on the first afternoon for just 133 and by the close of play Cambridge were 181-4, with Tom smashing 68 in less than an hour. The Light Blues went on to 361 on the second day and appeared certain winners. Oxford batted with much more conviction in their second innings, but in the end Cambridge needed just 20 to win and lost only one wicket in the hitting off the winning runs. The result meant future brothers-in-law Reg Bettington for Oxford in 1923 and Tom for Cambridge in 1924 had led their respective sides to victory in successive years.

Tom's overall batting effort for the Light Blues was very solid, with 625 runs in 20 innings at 32.89, and there were a further 243 runs for Somerset. But his best efforts were for Cambridge. His captaincy won praise all round. In *The Cricketer,* Digby Jephson wrote: "The captaincy of Lowry was a perpetual joy to those that understood the old-time game. There was no fuss – no needless shifting of a well-placed field, no hesitation. One could feel in the pavilion the strong magnetic influence of the one man over ten." Robertson-Glasgow thought "he was a leader in a thousand – versatile, strong courageous. His comments on the run of play would alone have justified the entertainment tax."

5. Percy Chapman (and Beet)

London, 1956: a sense of anticipation tinged with wonderment settled on Peter Lowry as he entered Lord's Cricket Ground for day one of the second Ashes test between England and Australia. Peter, Tom's nephew, was the son of Ralph Lowry. He had been invited to Lord's by his Aunty Beet (Chapman) as a special treat before entering Sandhurst Military College to begin a career in the army.

As the nephew of Tom Lowry and Percy Chapman, the hallowed inner sanctum of Lord's was thrust open for Peter and the famous names of the past were overwhelmingly charming when introduced to this upstanding young man, just 18. Peter remembers well sitting next to Bill O'Reilly in the Lord's dining room before moving to spend time with Jack Hobbs. As play progressed in the afternoon session, he was taken by former England captain Freddie Brown to view the commentators' box and it was on the way there that he sighted Percy Chapman.

"I saw Uncle Percy, but I was not allowed to talk to him and therefore never met him. Freddie Brown thought it best I didn't speak to him as it was better to remember him the way he once was, and not full of booze."

Tom, in his halcyon Cambridge days, had become particularly close to two people. Not only were they integral to his social circle but, amazingly, they eventually became part of the Lowry family. One was Reg Bettington, a hugely talented and popular Australian sportsman, who would eventually marry Tom's younger sister, Marion. The other was Percy Chapman, an Englishman who was destined to captain his country (at the same time as Tom was captain of New Zealand) and who would one day marry Tom's other sister, Gertrude (but known always as Beet).

While all three excelled at cricket, the outlet that brought the trio together, there were numerous other reasons for their commonality: they were rugby players; they were immensely talented at a range of others sports, including tennis and golf; they were studying at university (although only Reg with any real purpose) – Tom and Percy at Cambridge, Reg at Oxford; and above all they were "players" after stumps were drawn, starters for a drink or two and always good for a lark. It was almost inevitable that Tom and Reg would hit it off as fellow colonials, standing up to English stuffiness, but, perhaps more

Jack Hobbs, 197 first-class centuries to his name and dining companion of Peter Lowry at Lord's.

surprisingly, Percy was just as matey and took to their lifestyle and antics effortlessly.

Arthur Percy Frank Chapman, as he was christened, was born in 1900, two years after Tom. His biographer, David Lemmon, says he was imbued with the spirit of cricket from the age of three, and as one family friend was to write 25 years later, "a more delightful kid never breathed". Lemmon went on: "The boyish nature, the boyish enthusiasm and the boyish desire to play stayed with him for most of his first-class career, so that a New Zealand newspaper could write in 1930, 'To Percy Chapman cricket is a game and nothing more. He plays it now as he played when a lad at Oakham Preparatory School.' Not only was he a precociously talented cricketer growing up, but a bubbling, physical, charming extrovert."

By the time Percy reached Cambridge in 1920, his cricket deeds had captured headlines and become legendary. At Uppingham Public School, he had scored two centuries for his house in one afternoon. He achieved the first for the senior team to help them win the senior final, and then cycled down to the "middle ground", where the junior final was being played. When he arrived there were more than 100 runs needed for victory and only tail-enders left. He farmed the bowling, scored his second hundred of the afternoon and guided the juniors to victory.

By 1917, he was being noticed in the Public School reports in *Wisden:* "The outstanding feature of the season was the batting of APF Chapman, a punishing left-hand batsman who scores freely all round the wicket. He did not find form at first, but his last five innings were 66, 206, 160, 81 and 114. In four of these he was not out and the remaining innings – the 81– he was run out. He finished with an average as follows: 10 innings, 668 runs, four times not out, average 111.33. No doubt this must be a record for the school."

In *Wisden* the following year, he was named as one of the five Public School Cricketers of the Year, an innovation in cricket's bible to compensate for the absence of the Five Cricketers of the Year during war-time. *Wisden* described him as "a left-handed player, and he is one who is able to put great power behind almost any stroke with very little apparent effort... Chapman has a fine wrist and any amount of strokes all round the wicket." In this 1918 season he averaged 52. In his last season at Uppingham, he scored 637 runs at 70.77 and took 40 wickets. It may have seemed too early to envisage a path to the England cricket team, but some close and perceptive observers were predicting exactly that.

Percy's first year at Cambridge in 1920 coincided with Tom's arrival at the university. Tom, as already explained, could not make the first X1, but there were numerous opportunities to play together. In addition they were on opposite sides when Tom was turning out for Somerset. Percy had graduated to the Cambridge X1 in his first year and was to play for the following three seasons although, because of the dominance of the Ashton brothers, he never got the opportunity to captain the side. Tom captained the side in 1924, after Percy's departure.

The two very rapidly garnered a reputation for after-match antics and had many a wild night together. Former Sussex captain Tom Pearce recalled an evening at the old Palace Hotel in Southend when Lowry lifted and carried to the first floor a stamp machine and letter box which stood on the ground floor. Next day it took four members of the hotel staff to carry it back to the ground floor. Another report had Tom standing behind the stumps after a particularly good night and just allowing the ball to hit him, after which first slip would come forward, pick up the ball and return it to the bowler. This was a reflection that Percy and Tom were amateurs, there was no money at stake and the joy of living took precedence over all else.

Taking on greater importance for Percy at this time was the fact that the Lowry clan – Tom's mother and father, and siblings – were now all temporarily domiciled in England. Ralph and Jim were at Cambridge with Tom, Marion was preparing for finishing school, which left sister Gertrude. As the fourth of the five children, Gertrude had not progressed many years before she acquired the name Beet, which remained with her for the rest of her life. This had come about after her three big brothers became conscious of how their sister, out of shyness, frequently blushed, and so teasingly nicknamed her Beetroot.

Now in England, Beet was studying at the London Conservatoire of Music, which gave her a convenient entrée to her brothers' social circle and consequently a whirl of parties and social engagements. While her early years may have been blighted by shyness, Beet (like her sister, Marion), as she grew into a young woman, was no shrinking violet, and this was the personality Percy encountered at the 1921 Cambridge May ball.

Beet's natural, outgoing characteristics appealed to Percy. She had great potential as a golfer, a sport at which Percy was becoming increasingly adept (and at which Beet was eventually probably the superior player). She genuinely enjoyed the sports exploits of her brothers and had no trouble holding down a conversation within "blokeish" company, although she was converted to a cricket-lover only during her time in England. Over the next 18 months there were further encounters between the couple and by the time Percy and Tom toured New Zealand with Archie MacLaren's MCC team in 1922-23, the partnership had matured sufficiently for them to announce their engagement at a family gathering at Okawa.

Before this, Percy continued to attract widespread interest in the cricket world. In the 1922 university match he scored a cavalier century to ensure an innings victory for the Light Blues. This was followed by 160 for the Gentlemen versus the Players, equalling a record for a century scored in both matches. After Cambridge he returned to Berkshire to play minor counties cricket, one time hitting 10 sixes in an innings of 78. About this time came the first signs that his desire for social company and good times might eventually lead to a destructive lifestyle. David Lemmon said of him at this time: "The world smiled upon him and he smiled upon the world. He was blessed with that style of batsmanship that never fails to charm. He was delightful and daring. In action he gave the impression of being an exceptionally happy man, but that is the way some men hide their unhappiness and loneliness. The constant seeking of pleasure and of friends is often a desire to escape from the imprisoned sorrows of oneself."

By the end of the 1922 season, Percy was widely expected to make the MCC team to tour South Africa, but, after being surprisingly omitted, won a consolation selection (with Tom) in the second MCC team named for the winter, a tour of New Zealand under the captaincy of Archie MacLaren. While the chance to get to know Beet's homeland and visit Okawa must have held enormous appeal, it was his cricket performances that held sway and made him the hero of MacLaren's team.

In the lead-up matches in Australia, he impressed some hard-bitten critics. The team lost three of the these four matches, but Percy, who played eight innings, scored a brilliant century against New South Wales, plus five half-centuries. The Australian press described the century as "one of the most delightful exhibitions seen in Sydney for many a day. He made nearly every stroke from the long-handled drive to the short-arm hook...a powerful square-cut is his most effective stroke, but almost equally impressive were his drives past cover, and an occasional deflecting stroke to fine leg, all of which were marked by perfect timing and splendid footwork." The journalists were equally ecstatic about his fielding: "In all his actions he was delightful to watch. In covering ground, stopping and returning he was simply splendid....he soon became a public favourite and was heartily cheered."

Percy's ability to be everyone's friend, down-to-earth and always cheerful was soon put to the test on the Moeraki boat trip from Sydney to Auckland. David Kynaston describes in *Archie's Last Stand* how midway from Sydney to Auckland "the stokers went on strike, the ship lay becalmed for several hours and several of the team went down to do some stoking themselves, Chapman to the fore". Percy wasn't quite to the fore with the bat in the first two matches in New Zealand, but when MCC played Canterbury, he proceeded to tear apart a solid attack, scoring 183, and recapturing his Australian form.

20 A. P. F. CHAPMAN

Percy Chapman, the poise of "a young man of genius", ready to captain England.

There were no "test" centuries, but with 77 in the second international and 71 in the third, plus 108 against Auckland, he confirmed his status as the superior batsman of the tour.

Along the way, Percy's friendship with Tom grew. During a mid-tour break the pair spent some days at the Burdon property in south Canterbury. The Burdons were landowners on a par with the Hawke's Bay Lowrys. On another occasion it was noted in lunchtime speeches that two other members of the MCC party, Chapman and Lowry, "would have been here but begged off to attend the Wellington races". Towards the end of the tour, the Lowry family laid on lavish hospitality for the team while they were in Napier for the Hawke's Bay game. Tom couldn't play because of illness and Percy, perhaps with his mind on other things (like his impeding engagement to Beet), failed in both innings.

The long tour ended with further matches in Australia. Percy just missed another century against New South Wales when he was dismissed for 91, and scored 134 against South Australia. In all, he scored 1500 runs at an average of 56 on the tour. His aggregate was about 500 runs ahead of the second-highest scorer. Noting the "charm" of his strokes, the *Sporting Globe* remarked: "Yes, he is a great, lovable boy, a delightful personality, and a wonderful cricketer. When I remarked to him on Saturday that we hoped to see him out here again, he beamed and replied: 'I shall be delighted to come again if I get the chance. I have enjoyed myself immensely.'"

It was now almost a given that Percy would one day play in an Ashes series. His reputation

Percy and Beet's wedding day at Okawa in 1925. Back row: TH and Marsie Lowry, Jim Lowry, Mrs and Mrs Chapman. Front row: Leslie Taverner, Ralph Lowry, Tom (best man), Beet and Percy Chapman, Marion Lowry.

was confirmed in Australia (and New Zealand) and in England he was regarded as already capable of playing at the highest level.

With his amateur cricket on track, it was time to turn his attention to professional long-term employment (while also qualifying for Kent) and on his return to England he signed with a firm in Hythe, Kent, to learn the brewery trade. The consequences of this decision were indeed far-reaching.

Test selection soon followed. His debut was against South Africa in 1924, when he was still playing minor county cricket for Berkshire. At the end of the season he left with Arthur Gilligan's team to try to wrest the Ashes from Australia. Percy played in the first four tests and had a top score of 58. There were concerns about the tightness of his defence and his natural inclination to attack. He did manage to break one record. Taking up a Brisbane supplier's offer of as many oysters as any of the tourists could eat, Percy easily outstripped his team-mates by consuming 17 1/2 dozen at one sitting.

A mixed tour ended on a very happy note when he left Australia for Napier in March 1925 to marry Beet at Okawa. Tom was best man, Jim and Ralph groomsmen and Marion one of Beet's bridesmaids.

By 1926, England's barren run in Ashes series had extended from before World War I, and they had recorded just one win in 20 encounters. Percy was considered a pivotal part of changing those fortunes, but his influence came rather differently than expected. The first four tests of that year's Ashes series were drawn, with Percy omitted from the playing X1 for the fourth, a surprise given his good efforts in the previous two matches, including an unbeaten half-century.

There was an even greater shock when the teams reached The Oval for the deciding final test. Arthur Carr was dumped as captain, replaced by Percy. There was a public outcry about the decision – Carr was an astute, aggressive and admired captain, while Percy was still not a permanent England batting fixture. It would be only his 10th test and he was just 25, the youngest player to captain England in a home test. But, as so often is the case in these circumstances, a fresh face and voice can be the catalyst to success, and that's exactly what happened. England under Percy won the test and the Ashes.

Beet and Percy at their home in Kent.

The impact on English life was a revelation. This was the year of a huge general strike and the country was rather down in the mouth and racked by lethargy. Percy Chapman provided the morale-boosting antidote and the country celebrated joyously. Percy was hailed as "a young man of genius".

There was a telegram from the Prime Minister, a note from the King and when Percy and Beet were later in the year seen on the streets of London, a crowd gathered and there was clapping and cheering. Percy appeared invincible. But as David Lemmon related: "There were still years of fame to come – although even now the seeds of destruction, internal and external, were taking root."

In November, there was growing speculation in New Zealand that Percy and Beet were about to settle back in Beet's homeland. Given Percy's recent success as England captain, the idea seemed preposterous, but appears to have come about because Beet had been suffering from ill-health and because Percy now had his name on a land title at Okawa (a wedding gift), leaving the impression of possible re-settlement.

It was left to TH to clear up the matter in the *New Zealand Herald.* He denied "APF Chapman would settle in New Zealand" and, "a fortnight's trip abroad had improved Mrs Chapman's health considerably, and there has been no talk of Mr and Mrs Chapman coming to New Zealand". Percy and Beet were feted wherever they went. Beet's appearance and dress were noted in fashion columns. Described as a "tall and elegant beauty", she matched her husband in social graces when attending matches and functions.

For Percy there were still cricket fields to conquer. After his triumphant Ashes success, his cricket for a time was a little more intermittent because of travel and injury, but he was an

Percy and Beet Chapman at the home course at Hythe in Kent with Tom in tow while touring in 1931. Percy and Beet second and third from left, Tom far right.

automatic choice as captain for the 1928-29 defence of the Ashes in Australia. The significance of this series was the emergence of Don Bradman in test cricket (although he was demoted to 12th man in the second test) and the 4-1 series win by England.

Percy's inspirational captaincy was always apparent, most notably through the loyalty he engendered in the team and their desire to do well for him. With a 4-0 lead in the series, he surprisingly stood down for the fifth test, which resulted in Australia's only win.

Yet again he was inconsistent with the bat, with a 50 in the first test his best effort. The crowds loved his free and easy spirit and were full of admiration for his fielding. Australian wicketkeeper Bert Oldfield said: "Unquestionably he was the greatest all-round fieldsman I have ever seen."

Percy had now captained England in seven tests and won them all, but this proved to be the pinnacle of his career. The end of the tour coincided with another Okawa wedding, this time Tom's sister, Marion, to Reg Bettington. The cricket brothers-in-law wasted no time in donning some pads in a match arranged by Tom between his Moawhango club and Herb McGirr's Wellington team. One of the locals, Mick Horton, was ordered to bring two hogs heads of beer and place them on the end of his lorry tray, with the taps turned towards the players. Relaxed by the beer and a sumptuous lunch, Percy scored 109, Tom 42 and Reg 23. It was the only time all three played in the same side.

Captain again for the Ashes series in England in 1930, Percy scored a magnificent 121 in the second test and brilliantly caught Bradman in the same game. He had averaged 45 after four tests, by which time the series was level at 1-1. Then he was dumped from the captaincy, causing as much controversy as when he took over from Arthur Carr in 1926. England lost the fifth test and the Ashes.

Percy, before his dropping, had been named as captain of the MCC team to South Africa. He seamlessly overcame his axing and was accompanied by Beet on his last tour as England captain.

On the way to South Africa, Beet proved a treasure. She held her own with the men at deck tennis and played the piano, stomping her way through an endless repertoire of Gershwin songs. The team lost the series and Percy found runs hard to come by. But the Chapmans had a great time.

The social whirl continued on their return, and they were seen at Ascot races, society weddings and important golf occasions.

Percy entering middle age.

As the 1930s progressed, it became clear that Percy was not the cricketer of old, and that his life had become dominated by his desire for company and alcohol. His weight ballooned to 16st. He continued to captain Kent and played until the end of the decade, but as David Lemmon noted: "Towards the end of his career, the legend grew that he would sometimes leave the field for a few minutes. Many suspected, from the regularity of the occurrences, that the need to leave the field was allied to his need for a drink." As far back as 1928-29 on the Ashes tour of Australia, he was known to take a drink in the lunch break, although this wasn't unusual for cricketers of the time with bowlers, in particular, often choosing a pint or two to sustain them through the afternoon. Lemmon added: "The social intercourse of his cricket life was an integral part of his business life. As captain of England, a famed sportsman, he was a valued representative for a distinguished whisky manufacturer. As a representative, the opportunity, indeed the need, to drink became an imperative."

This decline in Percy's ability to cope without drink inevitably led to a parting of the ways with Beet, who could take only so much. There were occasions, mostly at Lord's, when he became something of a nuisance, wanting to drink with some who wished to watch or talk. He became a person to be avoided. But not everyone abandoned him and various old team-mates and members of the press treated him with kindness and respect. They remembered the deliciousness of his batting, his inspiring leadership and his sheer charm as a young man. The Adonis figure had now been replaced by a sad and tragic shadow of his glory days.

If Percy had never grown up, the reverse was true for Beet. Still in Kent as the war progressed to the Battle of Britain, she joined the YMCA, driving a mobile canteen (supplied courtesy of her parents) to nearby troops and airfields and began a new phase of her life, very much aligned to her mother's example of helping others.

Her work in the mobile canteen had extra meaning because based in Kent was the 2nd New Zealand Echelon, which had been diverted to England while on its way to Egypt, because of the feared invasion of England as an aftermath of the Battle of Britain. Lt Colonel Haddon Donald remembered her as the most charming of women, "so cheerful and helpful that everybody knew and loved her", as she drove around supplying troops with the comforts and the necessities of everyday life.

Most certainly the senior Lowrys were still in a position to help the war effort (as they had in World War I) and in an unprecedented gesture they effectively secured an occupation for Beet for the rest of the war.

This was a donation by the Lowrys of £10,000 ($850,000 in today's terms) to the New Zealand Patriotic Fund. Her friend, Peg Vivian (née Robertson), speculated in later life that the donation may have been because TH wanted to give her something to do soon after she had left an unhappy marriage. What could not be disputed was the patriotic gesture of the senior Lowrys and their record of generosity in two world wars. Presumably the Lowrys' Australian properties were doing well at the time because the donation (the largest individual patriotic gift made in New Zealand during the war) came in the form of Union Bank of Australia cheque. The £10,000 cheque was earmarked by the Fund Board for what became known as the "Lowry Hut", at Maadi Camp in Cairo. The size of the donation made it possible to build a superior type of welfare institute for the troops.

Whether TH had an ulterior motive or not, so firm a connection had Beet made with the 2nd Echelon officers and troops that it became her ambition to sail with them to Egypt. So in January 1941 she boarded the Duchess of Bedford (the only woman on board), together with her truck, and sailed for Egypt. The timing was perfect. The Lowry Hut was almost ready for opening and after arriving at Maadi in early March, Beet was able to be present at the Lowry Hut official opening by General Freyberg's wife, Lady Barbara, in July.

The Maadi camp had two YMCAs, the Central Hut and the far more salubrious Lowry Hut. The connotation of "hut" is misleading. Alex Hedley, in *Fernleaf Cairo*, described the Lowry Hut as "designed in accordance with desert conditions; it had an arched entrance to the patio and main door, and was built around a large outdoor auditorium cum lounge (which could accommodate 880 men) with numerous rooms to the side for amenities". These rooms housed a barber shop, sleeping quarters, a larger kitchen, conference rooms, library, billiards, table tennis, photography and other activities. The churches also used the facilities, holding communion services and, on Sunday evenings, song services.

During the war 76,000 New Zealand troops were stationed at one time or another at Maadi camp and most would have sampled the amenities and hospitality of the Lowry Hut.

While Graham Potter was the overseer of the Lowry Hut, Beet was a kind of hostess, greeting guests, sorting out problems, but refusing to be confined to the base camp. Haddon Donald described how, in her trusty van, she would turn up in the most remote places in the desert and be welcomed with open arms. Haddon said: "It seemed that anything we wanted she could provide and she would also send off telegrams to our parents to say we were okay."

There were others who were won over by Beet's easy charm and manner. During her time at Maadi, Lady Freyberg wrote to Beet's mother, Marsie, in Hawke's Bay: "I am so glad to take this opportunity of telling you what a delight it is to me to have got to know your dear Beet. She is a joy to all of us and has this wonderful capacity for radiating sunshine and

Beet Chapman geeing up the troops at Maadi in Egypt.

Entrance to the Lowry Hut, Maadi, Egypt.

The TH and Marise Lowry donation to the New Zealand patriotic fund paid for the Lowry Hut at Maadi.

Beet Chapman (left) in Italy 1944, with close friend Peg Robertson, who was soon to marry cricketer Giff Vivian.

LEFT: Beet Chapman in uniform while in Egypt.

happiness wherever she goes. It is quite enough for her to come into a room and smile and make everyone feel better. She has done and is still doing grand work and her value as a morale-raiser to the NZEF has been beyond price. I'm afraid that you and Mr Lowry must miss her dear presence very keenly, but in lending her to the NZEF, with her splendid getting of the Lowry Huts and the magnificent work that is being done in and around them, you have indeed made a very wonderful contribution."

Beet was no longer the blushing young woman and had a capacity to win over both "brass hats" and "lowly diggers" with equal generosity of spirit. Graham Potter described her as a person with remarkable poise and intelligence who, while a personal friend of generals like Freyberg and Kippenberger, was universally loved by the troops she came in contact with.

There were others who were close to Beet when she became associated with the Women's War Service Auxiliary, nicknamed the Tuis by Lady Freyberg. One was Peg Roberston, who, by the end of the war, had become Peg Vivian after marrying one of Tom's team-mates, Giff Vivian. Peg got to know Beet even better when another Lowry Hut was opened in Italy, about 35 miles south of Bari. Beet was housed at the Duke of Sandro's magnificent estate, but she was the only woman and it proved to be a very lonely existence. Peg described the new Lowry Hut as very basic, "just Nissan Huts, with a library but not much else", and a far cry from the Lowry Hut at Maadi. "We used to go down for two weeks at a time to keep her company and work there."

The superlatives ran deep when Peg Vivian, in her 90s, recalled Beet from those days: "Wonderful, warm and a great sense of humour, wonderful hostess, just a wonderful person." After the war, Beet became godmother to Peg and Giff's daughter.

Beet stayed with the New Zealand division until the war ended, becoming one of its longest-serving members. There was one furlough back in New Zealand in 1944 when her father died. Beet had spent the best part of 25 years away from New Zealand and there was much conjecture about where she would live. Some speculated that she may re-marry – to the urbane Gubby Allen – but Allen was to remain a lifelong bachelor, married to cricket and his beloved Lord's. Peg Vivian said Beet was very fond of Nick Wilder, an officer in the Long Range Desert Group.

She met Percy just once more, in the year after the war, before returning to Hawke's Bay, although England was to become a frequent visiting place, with Lord's and cricket very much part of her always busy itinerary.

Her time with Percy scaled the heights and plummeted the depths, but in the end she held no rancour or bitterness. As she told David Lemmon: "I made some true friends in our cricket career in those 'amateur' days and those wonderful professional players Jack Hobbs, Herbert Sutcliffe, Frank Woolley and many more – I'm so grateful to have known them."

Percy Chapman's final years were lonely and sad. David Lemmon relates how weeks before his death he was visited by a couple of old Kent team-mates, Les Ames and Hopper Levett, with Percy insisting they should join him in a glass of beer. Percy himself was sipping from a half-pint. As they departed they commented to the attendant how good it was that Percy had been weaned off the hard stuff. "Oh no sir," he said ruefully, "that wasn't beer he was drinking. It was whisky." Percy died just past his 61st birthday, after what the newspapers described as a very long illness. Beet could only say he must have died a very sad man.

Beet Chapman remaining active with
a game of curling.

Beet Chapman, divorced from Percy, lived on to become a centurion and led a remarkable life after her efforts in the war. Much of this was focused on helping other people, as well as playing bridge and golf – she captained the Napier Women's Golf Club. Beet was a non-materialistic person whose focus was essentially humanitarian. In her last 30 years she lived very humbly on the pension and owned only two cars in that time. Most of the family believed she had virtually nothing. She was still driving a car at 95, hit her century in 2002 and lived a further three years. After her death, and much to the family's amazement, she left a substantial amount of money to her 14 nieces and nephews.

Tom had always looked out for Beet, sympathetic to her failed marriage with Percy and concerned she had never had the family she wanted.

Incidentally, Beet's close friend, Peg Vivian, the wife of Giff and mother of Graham, lived on into her 90s. While not always in robust health, she carried on in stalwart fashion after being told at the age of 60 she would be dead if she continued to drink a bottle of gin and smoke a packet of cigarettes a day. She died in January 2010.

RIGHT: Beet involved in later life with her beloved golf.

6. Reg Bettington (and Marion)

In the early 1920s another colonial, Reg Bettington, was captivating the sports and academic elite at Oxford University. Reg had many advantages, but at the time of his Oxford life they weren't of a monetary nature. While the Lowry boys may have been financially well supported by their parents through university, this was certainly not the case for Reg.

In fact, to survive he needed the benevolent assistance of an uncle. To further make ends meet, during the long summer holidays of 1922 Reg was tutoring, coaching and giving blood, an unusual but handy source of income. Extricating himself for a short time from this varied moonlighting, Reg went to the country with friends and found himself playing in a local cricket match. It was a stunning summer's day and, dozing off while lying back in a deck chair, his hat covering his face, he was suddenly awoken by a tug on his sleeve. A voice cried: "Tom, Tom, what are you doing here? You're meant to be back in New Zealand." Reg took off his hat and found he was staring at an attractive young girl of about 18, who was deeply embarrassed.

"Oh dear," she said, "I'm so sorry, but I thought you were my brother Tom." Reg replied: "My name is Reg Bettington and I know who you are. Your brother and I are great friends and are often mistaken for each other." The young lady was Marion Lowry, Tom's younger sister, and she made up her mind then and there that Reg was the man she would one day marry.

Reg was an Australian, born at Terragong, near Merriwa, New South Wales, on February 24, 1900. He had one brother, John, another outstanding sportsman, who was two years older. The Bettingtons were pioneer merino sheep breeders from the 1860s and the property where Reg and John were brought up was, in some respects, similar to the Lowrys'. It had a nine-hole golf course, a cricket pitch and a tennis court. This was a playground for sports development and the boys were encouraged to play competitively from an early age with whomever they could inveigle, including staff, locals and any English jackaroos to be found in the district. They excelled on this home playground, helped no doubt by the DNA inherited from their father, Jack, who played rugby and cricket for Guy's Hospital in London in the 1880s.

While the brothers were close friends all their lives, in their father's eyes John was brilliantly clever, while Reg was a dunce. Reg, however, was soon to show that not only was he no dunce academically, but that he was an exceptionally talented all-round sportsman. Attending King's School at Parramatta from the age of 11, he was almost immediately promoted to the first X1 as well as receiving a classical education in Latin and Greek. So good was he academically that when World War I began and teachers started exiting to war zones, Reg taught Latin and Greek to younger boys – excellent training for his future career in medicine.

RIGHT: Reg Bettington, left, and his brother John.

Reg showing the power of his shot-making.

Brother John went up to New College, Oxford, in 1917 and was joined by Reg in 1919. Cricket writer and commentator Jim Swanton later wrote of Reg: "A very tall, very dark young man strode through the New College gates. We watched in awe, another Australian, so different from us. We called him 'Nig'."

Just as impressed was Raymond Robertson-Glasgow, a more colourful writer than Swanton and a much better cricketer. Robertson-Glasgow stood at slip to Reg in his first English season for Oxford (and later played alongside Tom Lowry at Somerset). "Reg made the ball buzz like a top and at the moment of delivery there was a sharp snapping sound. There was an even sharper snapping sound when he asked for lbw or a catch at the wicket. A Bettington appeal brought all Sydney to the Oxford Parks. Six feet and three inches in height, he took a longish run, bowled with a looping trajectory: not flat, like so many of his sort. His performance was brilliant that summer of 1920. Length, flight, spin and persistence; he had them all; also a faster ball of vicious suddenness."

As well, Roberston-Glasgow had an intimate knowledge of Reg's batting capabilities. "As a batsman he was a straight driver who exacted the nimblest footwork from bowler and fellow striker. He had a weakness for short runs, especially to mid-off if [the fielder] had any tendency to corpulence. Sometimes these alarums went wrong and he shouted while running hither and thither: "Yes, no, yes, no; back up, can't you; yes... run-out, and that by a mile."

Other writers were known to have sampled his straight drive when he rocketed one famous shot into the press box at The Oval.

That 1920 debut year proved to be a vintage season in first-class cricket for Reg. He took 56 of his 61 first-class wickets for Oxford at just 15 runs apiece. Included in his Oxford performances was a hat-trick against Essex, when he took 5-48. He produced the same figures against Warwickshire. In the Freshman match there were figures of 8-48 and against Somerset he took 12 wickets in the match – 7-47 in the first innings and 5-42 in the second. He also contributed impressively with the bat, scoring 487 runs at 30.43, including 99 not out against Leveson Gower's X1 when Oxford University reached their second innings target. An extra ball was bowled, and he hit it for 2, but this could not be counted because the match had already been won.

In the same year he won his rugby Blue. He was a ranging forward in the Oxford pack, selected also for the accuracy and power of his left-footed place-kicking. To add to the cricket and rugby Blues, he gained his golf Blue, the first Australian to do so. It didn't stop there. He distinguished himself as a tennis player and swimmer and, given the time, would have been good enough to win Blues in those sports as well.

By then his father was subscribing to a press cuttings service. Reg, so mocked as a child, had, by virtue of his sports exploits, become well- known in Australia and Jack could boast of Reg's prowess from the sports pages of English newspapers.

Reg at the time he captained Oxford.

When Reg eventually met Tom Lowry, the two colonials instantly hit it off. They were physically powerful men, equally big hitters of a cricket ball and a golf ball. They were hard-nosed rugby players and natural leaders with a daring and sometimes unorthodox approach to the art of captaincy.

While the likes of Jim Swanton may have viewed Reg, in particular, with some awe, others held contemptuous thoughts about colonials. They regarded them as upstarts with dreadful voices and lacking in manners. The likes of Evelyn Waugh decried them as "hearties", daring to take a place in British society where he for one couldn't at that time. These attitudes gave the pair a reason to stick together, but most importantly they were Antipodeans from similar backgrounds taking on the world in a far-off country.

At times they lived a life of self-indulgence and could behave outrageously. But they were social animals out to have a good time. They were in their absolute prime.

While Tom and his other future brother-in-law, Percy Chapman, played many matches together (at Cambridge and on an MCC tour to New Zealand), in the case of Reg, it was

Bettington versus Lowry. By 1923, Tom had made the Cambridge X1 and he came up against Reg in the annual university match at Lord's. Reg was the Oxford captain. Team-mate Robertson-Glasgow said: "As a captain, we believed in him and because of Reg, Oxford was once more a team." Oxford had suffered heavy defeats by Cambridge in the previous two years, but under the inspired captaincy of Reg they extracted revenge, helped considerably when the pitch was ruined by a thunderstorm.

Robertson-Glasgow, who opened the bowling for Oxford, later described how Reg came up to him and said: "That's enough from you. Give me the ball." Reg took 8-66, including Tom's wicket for 3, and Oxford won by 227 runs. In 11 first-class matches in 1923, he took 61 wickets at 16.55.

Reg played first-class cricket in each year between 1924 and 1927, but his appearances were limited. There were just two in 1924, seven in 1925, two in 1926 and two in 1927. He was still capable of coming in and snatching a five-wicket bag, but at this stage his concentration was on his medical career. After departing Oxford, his plan was to practise at St Bartholomew's Hospital, but before heading to Bart's, he spent some time in Glasgow as an intern.

The city at the time was the slum of Europe and subject to widespread lawlessness. Reg said later that it had been a profound experience that helped to form his political ideology, which was old-fashioned Tory, though his beliefs softened considerably in his later New Zealand days.

By 1927, Tom had returned to England, not permanently, but as captain of the first New Zealand touring team to Britain, and there was soon another case of mistaken identity. Reg had been out with friends and, having already imbibed liberally, decided that they would all go and have more drinks at the Savoy Hotel. The doorman, on sighting this rather merry group, blocked their entrance. Reg with a roar demanded "out of my way", and knocked the doorman to the ground. After a melee ensued, the police were called and Reg found himself transported to the Horseferry Road cells for the night. He was taken to court next morning to appear on assault charges. The case began at 10am. "Name?" called the judge. "Tom Lowry, sir," replied Bettington. The judge peered at him, closed his papers, stood up and said: "Good God, let this man go at once. He's due at Lord's in half an hour."

There are two versions of this story and it seems down the years there has been some blurring of the facts. In the second version, the judge asks Reg: "Is it true that you drank 15 beers, a bottle of brandy and six ports?" Reg replies: "No ports, sir." Reg handed the first version down to his daughter Vicky and it is likely to have the most validity.

Meanwhile, Marion Lowry attended Ivy House School at Wimbledon and then moved to a Brussels finishing school that she hated. Marion and brother Tom had forged a special affinity, possibly because they were the youngest and oldest. Tom looked out for Marion and Marion reciprocated. Tom, even at this time, was hooked on horse-racing, with sometimes dire consequences as he plunged into debt.

At one point Marion was dispatched to beg her mother for money for herself, which she duly took to Cambridge. There, at an arranged signal, a bucket was lowered from Tom's room in Trinity College to his sister standing beneath the window and the money changed hands. The secret was never divulged.

Eventually Marion got a job, but not something either Marsie or sister Beet knew about or would have approved of. She began modelling hats for Molyneux the courtiers. Encouraged by a busy social life and a lot of attention, she scandalously dyed one of her curls blonde. Percy Chapman and Beet took a very dim view of this and ordered its removal. Beet said: "Marion, I want you to come for the weekend, but you mustn't tell the others what you do [hat modelling] and you must get rid of that dyed hair. I'm having a very important person to stay and he won't be amused." Marion enquired as to who the mystery guest was. "Reg Bettington," replied Beet.

Marion did not tell Beet that she had already met Reg Bettington years before. The night arrived. Wearing her most fetching hat, blonde kiss curl to the fore, she pirouetted into the living room. The famous guest hugged her warmly and she hugged him back and there were mutual cries of joy at seeing each other again. Percy and Beet took severe umbrage at not being told and wouldn't speak to Marion for the whole weekend. Reg, on the other hand, was entranced and a romance started.

By 1928, Reg was planning to return to Australia and decided to devote a season to Middlesex. He played the fullest season of his career, scoring more than 1000 runs at 39.92 and taking 74 wickets at 32.59. Against Sussex at Lord's, he achieved the double of 100 runs and 10 wickets, scoring 28 and 95 and taking 4-87 and 6-78. Then, batting for the Harlequins against the West Indies at Eastbourne, he notched 127 in a total of 676-8 declared, the biggest tally against the tourists that year. There was another century, 114 for MCC versus Kent. His batting was so good that summer he was a candidate for the Australian team at home against England in 1928-29, although his bowling, while full of guile, had lost some bite.

Back in Australia, Marion found it difficult to pin Reg down. She was still pursuing him with gusto despite other engagements and boyfriends. Early in 1929, they found themselves at Haddon Rig in New South Wales, the home of the Falkiner family. The Falkiners' daughter, Lucy, had married Jim Lowry, and was living in New Zealand and Marion had become great friends with her sister, Enid. After a dance, and in the early hours of the morning in the library at Haddon Rig, Marion played her final card. On being informed that Reg was to return to Sydney the next day to attend a social function, she said she was sorry that she couldn't accompany him because she had to return immediately to New Zealand.

Reg capitulated with a proposal for marriage. Mr Falkiner was duly awakened at 2am to be told the exciting news. He was understandably very cross at being awakened and strode into the library without speaking. He took a copy of *Who's Who* from the shelf, looked witheringly at Reg, read an entry and shut the book. "Oh well," he said, and returned to bed.

The subsequent engagement announcement excited a lot of interest, with photographs in the *Times* of London as well as various Australian papers. This was followed by three weeks of festivities at Okawa as Marsie took control. A large contingent of Maori leaders was invited to the April 11 wedding celebration. It poured, but there was an impressive crowd at Napier Cathedral to cheer on the happy couple. Brother-in-law Tom was in the wedding party with Lesley Hill (father of Sinclair Hill, the famous Australian rural grazier) as best man.

TH and Marsie, as generous as ever, bought Reg and Marion what was described as "a pretty white house" in Greenoaks Avenue, Darling Point, where they began married life. Reg was due to take up a partnership with leading Sydney ear, nose and throat specialist Herbert Marks, but this did not happen.

Another Okawa wedding: Reg and Marion Bettington, 1929. Tom is slightly obscured at the left of the back row. Next to him is TH. In the middle row, Marsie is next to Marion and Reg. Ralph Lowry is on the far right.

Dr Reg Bettington in his early days as an ear, nose and throat specialist.

Marks died suddenly just as the Depression was biting and Reg was confronted by the prospect of no work. He wasn't helped by his sports reputation, which was seen by some to preclude a caring vocation. Eventually he took up practice and moved into rooms in Macquarie Street.

There was less time for cricket, but in the 1928-29 season he was selected in an Australian X1 to play against the touring England team captained by his future brother-in-law Percy Chapman. Reg had been included after a number of withdrawals and notably he captured the wicket of old Oxford team-mate Douglas Jardine in both innings. He played once for New South Wales in the same season sharing a sixth-wicket stand of 120 with Don Bradman against Victoria in Sydney. Bradman made 340 not out in the total of 713-6, with Reg getting 40. There was one appearance in 1929-30 and three in 1931-32, when he twice captained his state. About this time, at the request of the Australian Cricket Board, he also performed a tonsillectomy on the Australian cricketer Archie Jackson. Jackson who was hailed as every bit as good as Bradman, died within two years from tuberculosis.

During this Sydney cricket phase, there were other players and issues for Reg to influence. Captaining the North Sydney club side he saw the emergence of one of the greatest bowlers of all time, leg-spinner Bill O'Reilly. As a fellow leg-spinner, Reg appreciated the needs and ambitions of his young charge and, as his club and state captain, did all in his power to assist O'Reilly's advance.

In *The History of Australian Bowling*, Reg is quoted as stating categorically to all within his hearing that the young O'Reilly, not yet a test player, was "the greatest bowler in the world". As captain of New South Wales, Reg later cleared the path for O'Reilly's advancement to test status. This was during the 1931-32 season after O'Reilly had, in a major shock, been dropped from the state side against the wishes of his captain. As they prepared to play Queensland with O'Reilly omitted, Reg announced he was unavailable, to ensure, according to Vic Richardson, that O'Reilly could be fitted in. This was confirmed later by O'Reilly, who said: "Reg Bettington, a big, hefty, marvellous bloke, a real man's man, said to the selectors without a word to me, 'I'll get you out of this difficulty. I'm unavailable.'" O'Reilly then bowled well enough to be selected for his debut test against South Africa soon after.

In *The Time of The Tiger – The Bill O'Reilly Story*, author Dick Whitington described Reg's action in putting aside his own interests as "graceful and typical".

The following year Bodyline came to Australia and Reg and Marion were unwittingly pulled into the toxic maelstrom. Public enemy No 1, England captain Douglas Jardine, had an obsession about cleanliness and feared contamination from hotels, restaurants and almost any public place. By the fifth test in Sydney, Jardine was loathed and despised by just about every Australian. At this point the England skipper made a decision he would not stay at the team hotel and insisted to Reg that he wanted, with his wife Margaret, to stay at Greenoaks Avenue. So Marion would spend most of the day at the Sydney Cricket Ground with Margaret, before departing before stumps to get her back to Darling Point. Sometime after the end of play Marion would get a call revealing the exact time of arrival and Jardine would leap out of the car to avoid any following press and sprint to the front door before it was slammed behind him. Marion revealed that Margaret Jardine, especially, was constantly distressed by the predicament she found herself in as opprobrium was poured upon her husband.

Despite extending friendship and hospitality Reg, and also Beet Chapman, condemned the actions of Jardine and his use of Bodyline. Jim Swanton in *Sort of a Cricket Person*, said in doing so "Reg Bettington, a formidable Anglo-Australian sporting figure who had been a contemporary of Jardine's at Oxford wrote as 'a very close and valued friend'." Beet, in the meantime, took one of Jardine's bowlers, Gubby Allen, to task for sitting on the fence. Allen, a friend of Percy and Beet, as charming as ever, replied without committing either way.

A close friend of Reg at the time was the eventual newspaper magnate Frank Packer. Packer had returned to Sydney after a failed oil venture and was soon to become extremely fashionable. Packer was mad on horses, loved going to the races and became a breeder of note. He encouraged Reg into both and after the war they shared a mare called Belle Amber, which raced successfully at Randwick. Reg, naturally, wanted to make use of his New Zealand

racing connections and with the agreement of Packer, Belle Amber was sent to Okawa to be covered by Tom's prize stallion Faux Tirage.

If there was a lessening of Reg's participation in cricket, his skill on the golf course was regularly on display. He and his brother John won the 1929 state foursomes championship and three years later Reg won the Australian title in partnership with CH Fawcett. Even more meritorious in 1932 was his victory in the Australian amateur title at Adelaide after one of the most remarkable recoveries on record. Trailing his opponent, Harry Williams (the titleholder), by four shots with seven holes to play, Reg won the next six holes with a succession of five birdies to win 2 and 1.

Marion had also become an accomplished golfer. She and Reg became the first husband-and-wife team to win the state mixed foursomes title, going on to win three years in a row. Despite their success, in the aftermath of one tight victory at the 19th hole, Reg was critical of Marion's putting and a very long, mutinously silent train trip was taken after the win, with the handsome silver trophy sitting between them. Reg happened to be an expert putter, with deadly accuracy from eight to 10 feet.

Reg believed putting was 90 per cent confidence, "but the catch, of course, is to acquire the confidence". He said using the same method every time helped. "I find that overlapping with the left hand gives me a feeling of confidence. It enables one to steady the club with the heel of the left hand and putt with the right." Nevertheless, Reg could be known to get uptight on the course and Marion sometimes had to comfort and pacify his caddies in the face of barked orders and sudden losses of temper.

Remarkably, in 1932, he captained New South Wales golf and cricket teams. In an interview in the 1932 *Australian Golf and Tennis* magazine, he reflected on differences between the sports. "Playing golf," he said, "does not in any way have a deleterious effect on cricket form. But cricket is injurious to one's golf swing, mainly for the reason that in batting the wrists are kept in front at all times."

Reg had no doubt about the greater mental pressure of playing golf. "One might be a little nervous at the start of a big cricket match, but one soon gets worked up to concert pitch and the game becomes more automatic. In golf, however, there is a splendid isolation which does not apply to cricket. Every shot in golf has its own thought. I know of no more ghastly feeling than playing golf badly in front of a big crowd. There seems no escape from it, for it is only human to abhor making a fool of one's self in front of a large critical gallery. To add to the player's misery, too, the more he tries to pull himself together, the more hopeless he generally gets. In cricket a missed 'sitter' engenders much the same though, especially as the crowd generally rubs it in. Still generally an opportunity soon presents itself of making amends and all is forgotten, both by the player and the crowd. In golf, however, a man's misdeeds stay with him for the rest of the match."

Asked in the same interview why in 1932 his game had blossomed, Reg replied: "During the past 18 months I have been studying the game more closely. Some people say I have shortened my swing, but I do not know whether that is so. I certainly have endeavoured to accentuate the hitting from within-outwards theory, with the wooden clubs particularly. And,

LEFT: Reg won two Australian amateur golf titles.

as an important adjunct to this, I have concentrated on acquiring the weight transference from the right to the left leg at the moment of impact."

While Reg may have taken Marion to task at the 19th on that golfing day, he adored her always. She had kept up with him in golf, was an excellent tennis player, champion skier, was witty and outrageously funny, attractive, and introduced him to an eclectic world of people. The Lowrys became his family and he had only loose ties to his own. This may have been partly caused by the reconstructed Bettington family following the early death of Reg's mother at just 19. His father, Jack, re-married, to a 23-year-old and early on Reg had given up all his rights to the family property, Terragong, to his half-brother, with no money changing hands. An estrangement now existed with Reg and his family.

Reg and the Lowrys still had close ties to their English contacts and society and this was of no interest to a new generation of Bettingtons. Some of the Bettington clan may also have felt resentment at Marion's position in Sydney social circles, where Reg was a more than willing participant.

Amazingly, Reg still had a couple of first-class cricket games ahead of him. In 1938 he and Marion returned to England with the possibility of permanent settlement. Reg travelled by ship as a dentist-doctor, while Marion flew. On arrival he accepted an excellent position in Harley Street, coinciding with his Fellowship to the Royal College of Surgeons. Within a short time he was turning out for CS Marriott's X1 and for Free Foresters against his old university. In his two first-class matches (18 years after his first-class debut and at the age of 38) he took another five wickets to lift his first-class tally to 357 at an average of 23.79. His career batting record ended with 3314 runs at 27.38.

By 1939, it was clear Hitler was on the move, and the couple decided to return to Australia. The timing was impeccable. Refuelling in Frankfurt, their plane was surrounded by a large contingent of goose-stepping SS and, somewhat frightened, Reg and Marion realised how close war was.

Once home, Reg wasted no time in joining the Australian team of medics soon after war was declared, spending four year in various war zones, including Crete. Allowed a bible and a book of choice, Reg chose *Alice in Wonderland* and was photographed engrossed in the book in a dugout under an olive tree on Crete just before the invasion. By this time, Reg had lost much of his hair and the picture captures a balding figure with a daisy chain draped around his head. Here he also developed a passion for vegetable gardening. He was introduced to avocado pears and brought several home to Sydney with him, one growing very rapidly into a large tree at Greenoaks. Unfortunately, in 1950 a burglar used the tree to climb into the house, stealing Marion's precious pearl necklace.

Back in Sydney, Reg worked at Concord Repatriation Hospital, then the largest hospital in the southern hemisphere. But a change was imminent. The war had taken an undoubted toll and the chance to start a new life in New Zealand in the early 1950s was too good to let slip.

Marion, back at Okawa to visit her mother, noticed a vacancy for an ear, nose and throat specialist at Napier Hospital. Reg applied and was accepted. Their friends in Sydney were horrified the couple were heading to a "backwater" in New Zealand, but once settled, Reg loved it.

He had a large vegetable garden and his own kitchen and would set about bottling all the

Lord Cobham, the cricket-playing Governor-General, was a long-time admirer of Bettington.

fruit grown. He cherished the opportunity to resume his close friendship with brother-in-law Tom. This naturally led to more cricket at the Grove and for a time he coached the game at Hereworth prep school, including daughter Vicky's future husband, Gordon Thomas. His skill at golf was still regularly on display. There was also the annual Boxing Day tennis on the Okawa courts, where Tom's brother, Jim, was the recognised star. But Reg, with a peculiar shovelling style and as competitive as ever, would contrive to frustrate and exasperate Jim, who found his brother in-law just too much. Reg and Tom, meanwhile, had an added interest in Belle Amber after Frank Packer had passed to Reg his share in the mare.

Reg maintained his interest in cricket and when Charles Lyttelton (Lord Cobham) was

Governor-General of New Zealand (1957-1962), the two old cricketers met up after Cobham wrote what Marion later described as a fan letter. (Cobham was crazy about cricket and during his tenure played in a first-class match between the Governor-General's X1 and the MCC. His side included Martin Donnelly, Bert Sutcliffe, John Reid, Merv Wallace, Ray Lindwall and Gerry Alexander. Aged 51, Cobham scored 44 in the first innings.)

On a trip back to England with Beet in 1965, their first since departing in 1939, the Bettingtons visited Lord's and had lunch in the Long Room, where Gubby Allen was as attentive as ever (as well as providing rides in his Bentley). There were the usual photographs at the gate, where Beet took Reg's arm, and Marion who duly followed, laughed and said: "It was only fair." Reg had a wonderful visit to Bart's Hospital, and attended the Garter Service. It was the trip of a lifetime, reviving old memories, but in a vastly different country to the one he had left nearly 30 years earlier.

Back home, Reg continued to stay close to the Lowry clan. He got on with everyone. A nephew, Peter Lowry, described him as a marvellous man in every way – a big-hearted, friendly Australian with plenty to say. Peter was moved by the fact that Reg had looked out for him and his siblings after their father, Ralph, had moved on to his second wife and then his third. Another nephew, Tom Junior, used to share a mai-mai with him during the duck-shooting season and thought he was a lovely man.

Reg's life ended unexpectedly. On a miserable mid-winter's day in 1969, he left Napier for clinics at Wairoa Hospital and then Gisborne. After his usual hearty lunch at Wairoa Hospital, he hit fog and, possibly disorientated and a little sleepy, missed a vital turning on a treacherous road, plunging 100 feet to his death on to a railway track.

Marion lived in Hastings many years after Reg's death. Both Marion and Beet were accomplished golfers, each playing off a four handicap. Reg and Marion's only child, Victoria, married Gordon Thomas and today they live in England, where Vicky has been involved in charity work. Vicky always got on well with Tom, because "I was a precocious child and was never intimidated by his stern exterior".

7. New Zealand Captain

When Tom left Cambridge in 1924, he was an admired captain and an accomplished batsman, but he needed to make a living. Somewhere in the future was the likely inheritance of Okawa, and that's where he returned, together with Jim and Ralph, later in the year. But with TH still farming Okawa, it was time for Tom to branch out on his own. With the considerable help of the family he bought two farms close to Taihape – one of 2700 acres for £43,000 and 6000 acres opposite the Moawhango store for £60,000. The two farms became known as Pokaka (carrying three ewes per acre) and Burridge, and this is where Tom farmed for the best part of the next 20 years.

With his career sorted out, Tom smartly turned his spare time to his beloved cricket. He took over the captaincy of the Heretaunga club in Havelock North, leading the club from fourth on the table to a championship title in the following two years. Playing in Hawke's Bay made him eligible for the Wellington Plunket Shield team, but before he played any further first-class matches in New Zealand, he was whisked into the New Zealand team for a tour of Australia during the 1925-26 season.

He was by no means a first choice. The team was selected in October. However, four players – Stewie Dempster, George Dickinson, Syd Hiddleston and Dick Rowntree – become unavailable. They were replaced by Jack Banks, Hector Gillespie, Matt Henderson and Ken James, before Banks and Henderson also dropped out, allowing Tom, very much a third choice, to be included. Given the amount of cricket he had played back in New Zealand, his selection was based purely on reputation, but it proved to be a sound one. Tom showed throughout his career that given consistent match-play, particularly on tours, he would produce the goods.

In picking Tom for Australia, the selectors were keen to use him as a keeper, despite the belated selection of James. Tom kept in three of the four first-class matches, picking up four catches and three stumpings, two off his Christ's team-mate Roger Blunt's leg-spin bowling. Tom was in aggressive form against South Australia, smashing 123 in just 90 minutes, an innings that featured many of his favourite on-side shots. This century in the third first-class game of the tour was preceded by another big hundred in a minor game against Ballarat – 140 batting at No 3.

This was the extent of Tom's major cricket in 1925-26, although he scored 119 not out for Hawke's Bay against Manawatu in early April.

The relative success of the Australian tour encouraged the New Zealand Cricket Council to return to a long-held desire to make an inaugural tour to the home of cricket (and as it was always described then, the Home Country), England. At ICC meetings in London in 1926, New Zealand pushed its case and that May the MCC approved a non-test match tour for the

Tom, a late replacement in the 1925-26 New Zealand touring team in Australia. Back row: Rupert Worker, Cyril Crawford, Hec Gillespie, Charlie Oliver, Ray Hope, Tom, Bill Cunningham, Ken James, Arthur Alloo. Front row: Dan McBeath, Roger Blunt, Billy Patrick (captain), Frank Peake (manager), Ces Dacre, Cyril Allcott.

following year. But first there was the question of finance.

The council's 1926 balance sheet showed an excess of assets over liabilities of only £910, and with the cost of the tour estimated at £9000, the financial hurdle seemed excessively high. The NZCC, with enterprise not always notable in its long history, decided the tour should be financed by floating a public company. Authorised capital eventually reached £12,000 in £1 shares. Members of the stock exchange supported the float by agreeing to waive brokerage on any shares placed by them. Tom's father, TH, was at the forefront of a racing-cricketing fraternity on the share list. Between them, they owned most of the country's best race horses. TH owned Desert Gold, Jack Barrett, who had been secretary of the New Zealand Cricket Council from 1914-18, owned Count Cavour, George Greenwood owned Gloaming and Arnold Williams owned Rapine. This group, plus many cricket enthusiasts from all around the country, enabled the bulk of the capital to be subscribed.

During the 1926-27 summer, Tom put himself in the forefront of the selectors' minds with some punishing innings for Wellington in the Plunket Shield. There was 90 against Otago in the match starting on Christmas Day and later in January a near match-saving second innings of 110 against Auckland. With Tom having kept for New Zealand in Australia, the selectors were keenly aware he had two strings to his bow, which would prove useful for the balance of the team on a 38-match tour.

Nowhere near as certain was the position of captain. The *New Zealand Herald*, in an editorial at the start of the season, favoured Nessie Snedden, Billy Patrick or Dave Collins. "Among the players with minor claims to the position are TC Lowry of Hawke's Bay, who has

GOOD LUCK, NEW ZEALAND!

By
A. P. F. CHAPMAN.

Mr. Chapman, who led the England team that won back the Ashes last year, is a brother-in-law of Mr. Tom Lowry, the captain of the New Zealand team which arrived yesterday, and he toured New Zealand with Mr. A. C. MacLaren's side in 1922-3.

NEW ZEALAND has sent us several All Black sides to show us how to play Rugger, but never until now has she sent a cricket team to the Mother Country; and so more interest than usual should be taken in this pioneer band of men, only one of whom (their captain, T. C. Lowry) is known to cricketers in England.

Let us, then, straight away, wish the team " all the best "—good wickets, good weather, and good luck; in their own words, a very hearty Kia Ora.

From what I saw of them when touring New Zealand with A. C. MacLaren's side in 1922 and 1923, I think they will appeal to English cricket-lovers, and, given a good start and some easy-paced wickets in May, I am sure

thing in the shape of the heroic Nepia, of Rugger fame, she will be disappointed. There is one footballer, though—Cecil Dacre, their vice-captain, who plays for New Zealand at Soccer too. He is a really dashing bat who goes for the bowling straight away; and if he and Lowry get going together most of the runs will be in boundaries. They certainly won't tire themselves running between the wickets !

Dacre, who comes from Auckland, is also a very fine outfield, and can, so to speak, " pick up anything." This is essential in Auckland, for I remember that dogs seem to love to get through the pickets and stroll about the ground. This habit was very noticeable when we were there, and more so two years later when Victoria were visiting Auckland.

Percy Chapman drew on his personal knowledge of Tom and of New Zealand cricket to provide a tour preview for the *Evening News*.

also had experience in England..." But Tom was ultimately favoured by the NZCC policy of sending a young side to England and the *Herald's* candidates failed to make the cut – Snedden was 35, Collins 40 and Patrick 42. Tom, at 29, with an intimate knowledge of the English game and the benefit of touring experience, proved to be the perfect fit.

The selected team appeared to be useful in batting but deficient in bowling. Dempster, Blunt, Ces Dacre, Curly Page, Jack Mills and Tom himself were talented and, in some cases, proven players and all were expected to flourish with the bat on tour. But the bowling was thin in the fast/fast-medium bracket and leg-spinners Blunt and Bill Merritt (a criticised selection because he was only 18) would be crucial in the wicket-taking department. Cyril Allcott and Herb McGirr added to the mix as all-rounders. Ken James was the keeper, with back-up from Tom. Another useful addition would have been English professional Ted Badcock, then the coach of Wellington, but after he was selected for the tour, Auckland complained and he subsequently withdrew for "business" reasons, to be replaced by Bill Bernau.

The travel contrasts to today's international tours couldn't have been more marked. There was no fronting up at Auckland airport, embarkation with a turn left at the curtain, two-hop, 24-hour aeroplane trip to Heathrow. Tom was used to travelling, but most of the others weren't. When they left Auckland on March 29, there was another month to go before they

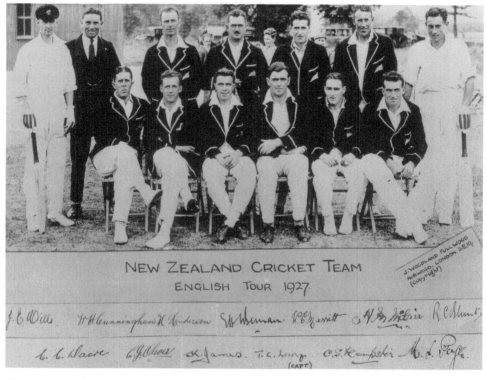

NEW ZEALAND CRICKET TEAM
ENGLISH TOUR 1927.

J.C.Mills   W.H.Cunningham K.Henderson   W.Truman   P.E.Yerritt   N.M.McGirr   R.C.Blunt

C.C.Dacre   C.J.Oliver   K.James.   T.C.Lowry   C.S.Dempster   M.L.Page
(CAPT)

Pioneers: Tom and his 1927 touring team to England.

arrived in England. On the SS Tahiti they sailed to San Francisco (with a stop at Rarotonga and a short-lived match against the locals, led by the King and up to 100 of his subjects), then a train journey across North America. There were stops in Chicago and Toronto, and a visit to Niagara Falls, before they were awed by the sights of New York. Then it was on board the Majestic (at the time the largest passenger ship afloat) for the voyage to Southampton.

Between Cherbourg and Southampton, Tom was interviewed by the English press on a radio-telephone link, first describing the team as "happy as sand-boys and keen to get to work".

"I realise this tour is a huge experiment...and there is much to be learned, and possibly unlearned. Our opportunities are nothing like so great. Ten years' cricket in New Zealand is only about equal to a season over here. The opportunities for practice are considerably curtailed. After 6 o'clock, it becomes too dark, as there is no twilight. Then again, matches take place only in Saturday. Yet the game is steadily forging ahead...it was felt the time had possibly arrived when a trip to England could be undertaken, not so much with the idea of achieving great success, but as an educational test, which would do great good to cricket in our little country down under."

The responsibility placed on Tom as captain was immense. Most of the players lacked international experience, the bowling line-up was inadequate and the fielding would prove well below standard. In addition, he had as manager Douglas Hay, a delightful man, but not travelled. At the beginning of the tour in London, with the side due the following morning

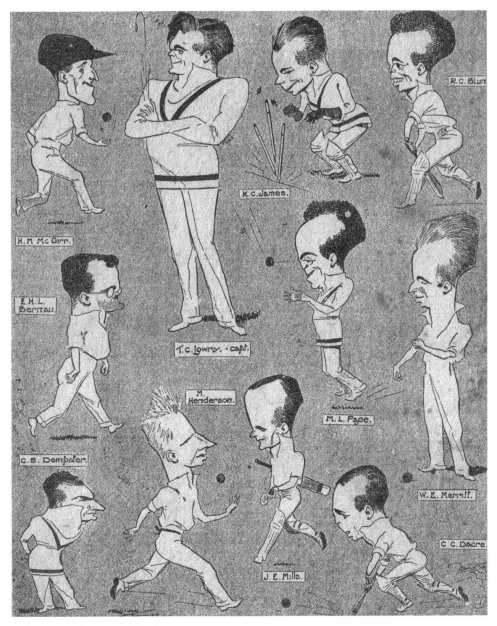

Another view of the 1927 team by an English cartoonist.

to take the train to Leyton for the Essex match, Hay in the dressing room said: "Now, you chaps, I want you all at the station in the morning on time, at least 10 minutes before the train leaves."

"What station, Mr Hay?" asked Tom. "The main station," said Hay. Tom replied: "I suppose you realise there are at least six main stations in London."

With Royalty at Wykeham Abbey. Princess Mary and the 1927 touring team. Back row: Herb McGirr, Stewie Dempster, Charlie Oliver, Ces Dacre, Bill Cunningham, Roger Blunt, Cyril Allcott, Curly Page, Ken James. Front row: Tom, Princess Mary, Douglas Hay (manager).

What Tom did have was an entrée into all aspects of English cricket. In the *Evening News*, a correspondent writing under the pseudonym, A Cambridge Friend, said of Tom: "His easy manner covers a forceful personality, and there are few men more capable of creating a contented side. If a touring eleven does consistently badly it is because it is not happy, and if it is not happy, look to the captain. We cannot be so Christian as to hope that the new arrivals will do consistently well, but we certainly do not wish them to do consistently badly. So everybody who likes free, resourceful cricket should be glad that the name of the visitors' captain is Tom Lowry."

During the early part of the tour, as the side sought to find its form, Tom was a tower of strength, using all aspects of his repertoire, from defending dourly to picking up the bowling by the scruff of the neck with a powerful, attacking innings. By the time he had completed his first seven first-class matches, he was averaging 60 and had scored three centuries. The first was against the MCC at Lord's, the opening first-class game.

Don Neely wrote in *Men In White:* "Lowry was no stranger to Lord's, but the rest of the New Zealand team took the field behind him like callow debutants." And that's how they performed in the field, dropping early catches to allow MCC to reach 392. But there was still much for Tom and the team to take out of the match. They proceeded to outscore the MCC in the first innings with a classy Ces Dacre 107 and a "refreshing, belligerent" 106 from Tom. Colonel Philip Trevor, writing in the *Daily Telegraph*, said: "Never have I seen him bat so masterfully and accurately." Set an impossible task of scoring 359 to win in 3½ hours, New Zealand still managed 224-4, with Tom top-scoring with 63 not out. There were 1502 runs scored in the match and the tourists won praise for their batting and style of cricket, but were fingered for their dropped catches and inconsistent bowling.

Their next match, against Essex, the first county game, was notable for featuring the first live radio commentary of a cricket match. It wasn't exactly scintillating. Pelham Warner was one of the commentators, and was described as having "a very quiet and ineffectual, apologetic-sounding voice", while his co-commentator was a former Essex player and now a preacher, Canon Frank Gillingham, known as Gilly. In contrast to Warner, he was an excellent speaker with a strong authoritative voice, but unfortunately his first broadcast coincided with a 20-minute break in play. After he had given a 10-minute description of the play so far, he became desperate for something to say. So Canon Gilly proceeded to read out the advertisements around the ground. Naturally the BBC was not amused, with advertising in any form strictly forbidden. Nevertheless, this was the forerunner to the famous and long-running BBC *Test Match Special* and a similar success story in New Zealand, *Summer Sports Roundup*. New Zealand lost this match, but at least Tom gave the commentators something to talk about, with fighting innings of 61 and 30.

Curly Page scored 140 and had a match-winning partnership of 129 with Tom against Worcester.

When the tourists arrived at Hove for the Sussex game at the end of May, they had still to win a game. Sussex were without their star bowler, Maurice Tate, and Tom led a merry run feast against a weakened attack. While the New Zealand top-order were all among the runs, it was Tom's 105 at a run-a-minute with 11 fours that hammered home the advantage. The *Times* said: "Lowry by the brilliance of his driving and the neatness of his cutting outshone his partner [Page]." The newspaper added: "It would be flattering to describe Lowry as being an elegant batsman, but of his efficiency, spirit and power there can be no question. He made some of his hardest hits firm-footed, but when the ball had to be reached he was very quick on his feet in getting to the correct place."

With a big first-innings lead, New Zealand bowled out Sussex in the second innings for 191 and it was a mere formality to knock off the 41 runs needed for their first win in England.

The Sussex game was followed by a drawn match against Oxford University and then Lowry's men recorded their second win, this time against Worcestershire. The county, like Sussex, left out their best bowler, Fred Root, but, batting first, New Zealand were disastrously 11-3. Tom, batting at four, was dropped before scoring, then stopped the rot with resolute defence, afterwards blossoming with some powerful shots in front of the wicket. His 74 (in 105 minutes), while slower than his normal run rate, still included 10 boundaries. While Worcester trailed New Zealand by only 54 on the first innings, a third-wicket second innings partnership of 129 between Tom and Curly Page sealed the match for New Zealand. Page scored 140 and Tom, in swashbuckling form, scored 106. He gave the outfield terrors as he hit the ball repeatedly in the air, and he was dropped off successive balls in the 80s by none other than William Shakespeare. On both occasions Tom lofted the ball down to Shakespeare, fielding on the North Road rails at long-on. The first went between his hands for four and the second dropped out of his hands. Tom was a reluctant teller of his own cricketing stories, but he always took some delight in relating his meeting with William Shakespeare. Tom declared at 349-5 and Worcester were bowled out for 209 to give New Zealand victory by 194 runs.

Tom's terrific, lead-from-the-front start to the tour was a compelling factor in ensuring the disparate members of the side worked cohesively as a unit. The team was a mixed bag socially and in character. Tom himself had a kind nature and while he could be blunt, he related to all backgrounds. His old Christ's team-mate, Roger Blunt, had a superior air, and was polished, urbane, fastidious and sometimes more English than the English in speech and manner.

Bill Cunningham had a troubled tour in 1927.

Opening batsman Jack Mills carried himself in similar vein to Blunt, and batted with his shirt buttoned at the wrist and the collar. Bill Bernau, like Blunt, was academically strong (a qualified lawyer and barrister), but carried a grudge against the world, exacerbated by a love affair that had gone wrong (he received a Dear John letter from his fiancée while on tour), and could be difficult. Lifting the spirits would be Herb McGirr, who was always wise-cracking and never afraid to speak out. Ces Dacre and Stewie Dempster, befitting their cricket prowess, were both cocky and confident, while Bill Merritt had turned 19 on tour and was not long from selling newspapers on the streets of Christchurch.

Then there was another Canterbury player, Bill Cunningham. In a ship-board photo of the team on the way to England, the Canterbury fast-medium bowler Cunningham squats in the front row, with a boyish, joyous grin on his face. Vice-captain Ces Dacre described Cunningham, in the early stages of the tour, as the wag of the party. This was soon to change. When New Zealand had toured Australia in 1925-26, Cunningham was easily the best of the bowlers, taking 37 wickets while forming a close friendship with Tom. Naturally he was expected to be major player in England.

But Cunningham played in a paltry seven of the 26 first-class matches for a meagre five-wicket return and for this state of affairs he blamed his captain. Cunningham was a trade unionist, and his father was from Ireland. He believed Tom, the Hawke's Bay aristocrat, was prejudiced against him. Cunningham later related a story to Dick Brittenden about when the team was playing in Wales. Tom, talking to one of the hosts while Charlie Oliver was batting, said that Oliver "comes from the same district as this fellow here", waving at Cunningham sitting nearby. Cunningham replied in a loud voice: "At least we didn't steal land from the Maoris."

But in the Brittenden interview, Cunningham failed to explain some of his antics in Australia and England that may not have impressed his skipper. On the Australian tour at an official luncheon for the New Zealand team hosted by the Lord Mayor of Adelaide, he downed the best Australian wine, provided in quality glasses, in one gulp as though it was a pint of beer, with accompanying, unrepeatable comments. There were other, possibly apocryphal, stories of Cunningham that showed his lack of respect for authority. At Lord's, the New Zealanders met King George V. Cunningham maintained that "Lowry tried to bar me". Cunningham said the King was sitting in a wicker chair in the Long Room. "He nearly fell off his chair when I walked up and said, 'Cunningham of Canterbury' to him. His reply was, 'Sit here Cunningham, I want to have a talk with you'."

What could not be denied was that Cunningham appeared to have completely lost the ability to bowl, suffering from a classic case of the yips. A later New Zealand player, Mark Richardson, who famously changed from left-arm spinner to opening batsman after suffering the same symptoms, said that if Cunningham was anything like himself it would have been a matter of "never being able to trust yourself that you could do it again". Richardson also added that he was never deprived of opportunities to come right but "it was as if they were giving me enough rope to hang myself".

Cunningham's case of the yips may have been a result of having the umbilical cord severed from Billy Patrick, his Sydenham club, Canterbury and New Zealand captain. In each team, Patrick directed him almost ball by ball as to what he should bowl. Just before the start of the England tour, Cunningham had bowled poorly for New Zealand in matches against the Melbourne Cricket Club. After arriving in England, Tom seemed to confirm a lack of confidence in the Cantabrian by playing him irregularly. Some thought the problem was muscular, others ventured to suggest it was more a case of the head. As matters progressively got worse, vice-captain Ces Dacre was deputed to take Cunningham to Lord's so that the England professional Patsy Hendren could have a look at his bowling action.

Dacre later explained what happened: "Cunningham was a little upset when I informed him about going to Lord's for practice and he promptly went back to the hotel and sat down for the rest of the morning. After some persuasion, I got a taxi and off we went to Lord's to see the famous Patsy Hendren and his cure for our best bowler, but it was no good. Poor Bill was hopeless. He got so bad one could not bat in the nets against him."

Some of the subsequent stories of Cunningham's treatment and performance in England were sheeted home as Tom's responsibility. It seems unquestioned that both took a firm view of their station and philosophy in life. Tom from aristocratic stock, a no-nonsense, natural leader of men; Cunningham from the other side of the tracks, proud, working-class, trade unionist and adamant believer in the position and rights of the working man. Yet, Cunningham was every bit a trade unionist while on the 1925-26 tour of Australia, when the pair were close friends.

The 1926 general strike in Britain may have hardened attitudes on both sides, and most certainly at this time (and beyond) English cricket was beset by snobbery and bigotry. Amateurs and professionals changed in different rooms and took the field through different gates. The pro was the servant and was frequently treated in a sort of benign, good-humoured fashion. But in the end it appears Tom completely lost faith in Cunningham's ability to bowl effectively and take wickets, and in an era devoid of team psychologists, no-one could crack the code to bring the bowler back on song. Almost as soon as the Brittenden interview appeared, other team members let the distinguished writer know that Cunningham had been hard to manage and that he had brought his apparent banishment on himself. If there were underlying tensions caused by the Cunningham's demeanour, the *Times* of London failed to detect them when it said "[New Zealand are] extremely lucky in having TC Lowry as captain. They have

Princess Mary with Tom and English cricket identity "Shrimp" Leveson Gower.

avoided all those stupid little frictions which are incidental to so many tours, and on the field they have consistently given of their best."

Tom's own form in the middle part of the tour slumped. After the Worcester game at the beginning of June he took nearly a month to regain his batting momentum. Striving to regain touch he employed a much more restrained approach and eventually at Bradford he occupied the crease for two hours and top-scored with 48 against star-studded Yorkshire, whose ranks included Wilfred Rhodes. Tom continued to bat in a contained fashion in the next game, against Nottinghamshire, again top-scoring with 74 in a rain-affected draw. By the match against Gloucestershire in August, he was back to his attacking best, batting just 85 minutes for an unbeaten 101. This was followed by 81 against Derbyshire, the tourists scoring 541-9 declared, their largest total of the tour, to record their biggest win, by an innings and 240 runs.

When not batting, Tom spent the tour endeavouring to get the best out of his limited resources at the bowling crease. His methods were based on originality – the frequent use of his medium-paced attack at one end, with spin at the other and often at the start of an innings, and by a constant inter-change at the bowling crease. Not everyone liked his approach. Tom Reese in *New Zealand Cricket* said: "Lowry got the other side out cheaply despite his too frequent bowling changes." And he could be tough on his players. Early in the tour Tom put Merritt on for one over to enable two other bowlers to change ends. Merritt promptly muttered that it was the wrong end. Tom immediately took him off and fielded him in the deep at both ends of the ground for more than an hour, after which he put him on again at the wrong end. Merritt had learnt his lesson and said nothing, so after one over he was switched to the favoured end. Throughout the tour he handled Merritt superbly, always trying something different, and the youngster responded by taking 107 wickets in first-class matches.

Where Tom had greater frustration was with the pace attack and the bowlers' inability to place the ball where needed. He would complain loudly that if he asked one of the bowlers to ball six balls outside the off-stump or six balls outside the leg, they would find it impossible to do so. He never hesitated to try his own unusual bowling ideas to change the fortunes of an innings. Ken James related how Tom would use the full toss as a wicket-taker when a slight shower had temporarily held up play though not materially affecting the wicket at all. He would call out loud enough for the batsman to hear: "I think I'll have a bowl. I feel this wicket will take spin now." He would then make every effort to get one of his old-fashioned medium-paced off-spinners to bite. If one deviated an inch or two he would promptly say to the umpire: "I thought so. I'll bowl round the wicket, umpire, please." The batsman, unaware of Tom's abilities and methods, would start playing ultra-conservatively, watch the ball hawk-like, and, fearing the worst, become cramped in his methods. Suddenly Tom would launch a full toss straight at his chest, as fast as he could. Often, the inhibited batsman would react late, try to swing the ball to the square leg boundary, and get a top edge to one of Tom's judiciously-placed fieldsmen.

A better performing bowling attack would have certainly added to the right side of the tour results ledger. The medium-pacers Bernau, McGirr and Allcott all had their moments, but with regular lapses in length and direction, they couldn't be relied upon. The left-armer Henderson was found wanting in most aspects and, of course, Cunningham was a disaster. It was left to the leg-spinners, Merritt and Blunt, to carry the major load – Merritt taking 107 wickets at just 23.64 and Blunt 78 at 24.97. Blunt could fairly be described as the star of the tour. In addition to his excellent leg-spinners, he topped the batting aggregate with 1540 runs at an average of 44, and was rewarded by being named as one of *Wisden's* Five Cricketers of the Year. *Wisden* confirmed him as the "finest all-rounder" in the New Zealand team and a "stylish and skilful batsman".

Blunt scored the most runs and was only marginally pipped for best average by Dempster.

Roger Blunt, who had an outstanding tour of England in 1927.

Tom was a clear third in both aggregate and average, getting his 1277 runs at 38.69. The strength of the team was all too plain to see in the batting figures, with Mills, Page and Dacre all also exceeding 1000 runs for the tour. Not only did they perform well, but the batting was marked by positiveness and attractiveness. Given the youthfulness of the side, it was a pity that the fielding lapsed so frequently with indifferent ground fielding and uncertain catching.

RIGHT: Practice at Lord's. Note the matting pitch.

Minhinnick's cartoon shows John Bull farewelling Tom at the end of the 1927 tour.

The bowlers' figures suffered from the fielding incompetence, but the bowlers themselves were among the poorest of the side's fieldsmen. Of the 26 first-class matches, seven were won, five lost and 14 drawn.

Despite the inadequacies, Tom, leading the way, and others had opened English cricket doors for the first time, and the hosts liked what they saw. As captain, Tom was universally praised. The English appreciated the way he always pushed for the win, and his encouragement and example in setting a "joyous and aggressive" approach to the visitors' batting. There were other touches. He insisted the players followed directly behind the umpires on to the field at the start of a session in the field and was equally insistent the incoming batsman had to cross the outgoing batsman on the field of play. They may have been small matters, but they were important in Tom's strategy to give county players a taste of what New Zealand could bring to the game. One cricket lover told writer Colonel Philip Trevor: "These New Zealand lads are real cricket lovers and that's what makes them attractive on and off the field. I've seen every team that has come to this country from every Dominion and every dependency. I've never seen one in which the spirit of cricket as a game lived so vitally as in this New Zealand one."

What the team couldn't do anything about was the appalling English summer, supposedly the worst for 50 years. The rain-affected matches had a deleterious impact on the tour finances. To build up the tour revenue, extra matches were arranged for the journey home, the first against All Ceylon in Colombo and then a first-class game against New South Wales at the Sydney Cricket Ground.

New South Wales, aware of the New Zealand's improving status in the game, stacked their team with test players and beat the visitors by 10 wickets. Tom kept wickets, getting two stumpings as well as scoring 44 and 35. The five-week sea journey had taken the sharpness off the team and it was no surprise they struggled.

The players had been away for seven months and were naturally bursting to get home, but first there was a shocking tragedy to deal with.

Aboard SS Tahiti, and still not out of Sydney Harbour, Tom and the team saw their steamship mowing down the Watson's Bay ferry steamer, Greycliffe. The ferry began to overturn and was broken in two, with Tahiti sailing through the ferry, which sank immediately. In fine, calm weather and with excellent visibility, 40 passengers died on the afternoon of November 3. Many were children. The tragedy stunned people because of its swiftness and horror. Because the Tahiti was still in the inner harbour, it's likely Tom and many team-mates were on deck and witnessed the catastrophe.

One crew member dived overboard to give assistance (and was later awarded a bravery medal) and other help was given. By 8pm the Tahiti, sure that it was undamaged, surprisingly sailed on to Wellington. There was controversy over this decision owing to the police's inability to question members of the crew (and to be sure the captain hadn't been drinking). This meant New Zealand detectives in Wellington were required to obtain statements from crew members some days later for a Marine Court of Inquiry. But the passengers' views, including those of Tom and his team, were never sought and were lost forever. Amazingly, newspaper reports of the New Zealand team's arrival home made no mention of the tragedy and a civic reception and parliamentary welcome proceeded as scheduled.

Tom, never one for pedantry, made his points effectively in reply to the various toasts, praising his batsmen, despairing of the fielding and showing caution in pushing for full test match status for future England tours. He was grateful for the "magnificent time given them. In the first match we walked on to the ground just like people about to take their first trip in an aeroplane. Perhaps there had been visions of dragons and supermen. However, we met with success and created interest."

Before disbanding, the team played the Rest of New Zealand in Wellington and Christchurch, the first partly washed out by rain with Tom scoring 80, the second easily won by the touring side, with Tom top-scoring with 78. There was an ironic twist on the last day's play of the tour. Bill Cunningham, the man who had given his skipper considerable angst, played for The Rest in the Christchurch match, and was last man out in the second innings, bowled by Tom to give New Zealand the win.

After eight memorable months of ground-breaking cricket, Tom headed back to his Moawhango farm. The shareholders of New Zealand Cricket Limited weren't so fortunate. There were no dividends and a good portion of their capital disappeared after the voluntary winding-up of the company. But what a magnificent investment they'd made in the future of the game in New Zealand.

8. Cricket Peak

A tour of England followed by a domestic New Zealand season starkly revealed the paucity of chances available for the leading players of Tom's ilk. In England in 1927 the tourists played 38 matches (28 first-class). In the next two seasons, Tom had the promise of a maximum of six Plunket Shield matches. There was also a mini-tour of New Zealand in the 1927-28 season by an Australian X1, meaning possibly another three matches for the leading New Zealand players. So an average of four or five matches a season was the meagre lot for even the best first-class cricketers. It's no wonder, then, that for much of the 20th century New Zealand cricketers were such late developers.

For the 1927 tourists, though, all was not lost. At the 1929 Imperial Cricket Conference in London, New Zealand was invited to send a team to England in 1931. In its annual report that year, the New Zealand Cricket Council stated: "It is not the general intention of the management committee that New Zealand teams should go to England at such short intervals as four years. It is felt that visits to England should, as a general rule, not be oftener than every six or eight years. However, the management committee is of the opinion that an exception should be made for our second tour, so that we may still have the services of some players who toured England in 1927."

Significantly, the committee added: "We must guard against the possibility of our young men playing so much cricket that their life's work may be prejudiced or affected. However, the committee, after consideration, is in favour of a tour in 1931."

This livelihood concern was not merely a whimsical judgement from a paternalistic governing body. A tour of England represented six months or more away from the work-place, and from wives and children. Players received a token daily allowance and, given some players would take leave without wages or salary, the commitment to tour was often fraught with conflicting interests. In Tom's case, he could leave a farm manager in charge and use family back-up, although when the 1931 tour took place a calamitous depression was still in progress, export prices had fallen by 40 per cent and many farmers, in ruin, were walking off their land. This was the time when Tom developed a life-long aversion to "working for the bank" and from then on, in times of economic downturn, he would loudly proclaim that it was time to "put the plug in" and everyone then knew that spending must stop.

In the years before the 1931 England tour, Tom devoted considerable time to cricket, playing his regular club fixtures, representing Wellington in the Plunket Shield and captaining New Zealand in the limited international matches available. This devotion to the game involved more than a simple drive to the local park. Weekend after weekend he would make the dreadful (at that time) Taihape to Hastings road journey to play his club cricket in Hawke's Bay (a round trip of 500km) and when he played occasional club cricket in Wellington (to help lift the quality of his preparation for bigger matches), he travelled to the capital on a Friday and back after the match – 470km.

None of this arduous travel seemed to affect his run-scoring. In the 1927-28 first-class season for Wellington, he was consistently successful – 81 against Canterbury, 46 versus Otago and then his highest first-class score, 181, against Auckland. Wellington were set 735 to win that match after being bowled out for 121 in their first innings, and managed 458 in the impossible run chase. He finished the season in April with a trip to Napier, where he scored 141 for Hawke's Bay against Wellington, whose ranks included Herb McGirr, Stewie Dempster and Ken James. He wasn't so successful in three matches (one for Wellington and two for New Zealand) against the visiting Australian X1, with 49 in the second unofficial test his best effort.

A pipe instead of the apparently mandatory cigarette. Tom, caught unawares before a day's play.

Quality opportunities were even rarer in 1928-29 – just three Plunket Shield matches for Wellington. He scored runs in every match, including 134 against Canterbury.

The opportunities may have been limited, but they revealed Tom at his cleverest with the bat – belligerent, commanding and consistent. Fortunately, just round the corner, there were more significant tours that would carry Tom's big-hearted imprint on the history of the New Zealand game.

The first was a tour by the MCC in 1929-30, for which Tom prepared by leading Wellington to another Plunket Shield victory. This campaign included a century against Auckland. The MCC tour had been facilitated by brother-in-law Percy Chapman while visiting the Lowrys after the 1928-29 tour of Australia, and while it wasn't what could be termed a full-strength side, it had such accomplished players as KS Duleepsinhji, Frank Woolley and Maurice Allom, and was captained by Harold Gilligan, after his brother, Arthur, had withdrawn because of illness. Three test matches were scheduled. That eventually became four when the tourists agreed to an extra match after the first two days of the third were washed out.

The New Zealanders who played in the series became our first official test cricketers (although they didn't know it when the matches were played because the status was granted retrospectively) and, of course, Tom became the first New Zealand test cricket captain. Until this time there were only three test-playing countries – England, Australia and South Africa. But in a four-year period similar status was granted to the West Indies, then New Zealand, then India. The relative success of the 1927 touring side did much to hasten New Zealand's elevation to this level.

Despite the initial unofficial status of the tests, there was intense interest in them and Tom, as captain, believed England could be beaten. Unfortunately, weather played a significant part in foiling his optimism, because New Zealand suffered by batting on a gloomy, overcast first day of the series in Christchurch. After winning the toss, New Zealand plunged to 21-7.

Tom the first victim in a hat-trick by fast out-swing bowler Maurice Allom, who also picked up a fourth wicket in the same over. Tom, Ken James and Ted Badcock were the hat-trick victims, with Tom joining the other two with nought beside his name (James and Badcock both got pairs in the match). New Zealand made just 121, but England struggled in reply, with Tom using all his wiles to curb the tourists. When Woolley arrived at the wicket, Tom soon introduced Curly Page's off-breaks, and when the left-hander was out, Page was removed, Tom not allowing his limitations to be exposed.

With England leading by only 69, all out before lunch on the final day (Saturday was lost to rain), New Zealand had a good chance of saving the match. Wickets again fell steadily, but Tom, while clearly not in his best form, battled away for 94 minutes as he courageously tried to play out time. This he did by picking up singles and the occasional four, and skilfully manoeuvering the strike. Ever his own man, Tom batted in a blue cap and while he defiantly kept out the English attack he was barracked by some spectators, disgruntled that he was not wearing his black cap. In fact, the cap was not of Cambridge origin, as the crowd thought; the blue was of his Moawhango club. If the crowd was in fickle mood, this was nothing compared to Tom's prickliness when George Dickinson, after defending well, unnecessarily lashed out and was caught at cover. Finally, with the last man in, Tom twice hooked Nichols for boundaries, but when he was bowled for a brave 40, England needed just 63 to win in 105 minutes, a task they accomplished for the loss of two wickets.

Maurice Allom, who bowled a sensational spell in the Christchurch test.

So the first test was lost, but after that New Zealand held their own in the tests in Wellington and Auckland.

In the Wellington test, Dempster and Jack Mills put on 276 for the first wicket, both getting fine hundreds and ensuring the match would not be lost. Tom batted at three in this innings, but as so often happens after an interminable wait, he lost his wicket cheaply when he was brilliantly caught by Duleepsinhji at slip from a late cut off the middle of the bat. Duleep, who eventually became the Indian High Commissioner to Australia and New Zealand, later remembered from the Wellington test playing a lucky hook shot off a fast short ball from Dickinson that still managed to hit the fence. Tom, in his favourite short leg position, immediately piped up: "Well played Duleep." He didn't miss a chance to encourage the shot again. But as Duleep recalled, after Tom had spoken, he decided not to repeat the stroke, Tom, on this occasion, meeting someone wise to his wiles.

Many of the English tours of this era encompassed visits to the provinces, and after the Wellington test the tourists played Hawke's Bay at Napier, where there was a chance to sample the hospitality of TH and Marsie Lowry. They were stunned at what they found at Okawa and Maurice Allom, who with fellow tourist Maurice Turnbull wrote a book on the tour, turned lyrical in describing being in Okawa's Poplar Grove: "The giant trees climbed up into another world which was alive with the notes and chatter of birds: the sun pierced through

and made the sphere below hazy with heat and quiet and sort of hollow for sound; strewn about the ground replete figures talked at moments in awed whispers."

But test duty called in Auckland. The third test, at Eden Park, was ruined by rain, with only one day's play possible. In the fourth tests, at the same venue, Tom again played a fighting captain's innings, scoring 80 which, by his standards, was a battling, protracted effort of 215 minutes. He rescued a New Zealand slump in reply to England's 540, ensuring the test would be drawn again. The great pity was that Tom's fervent hope of a test victory had not been achieved, but leaving aside the first test debacle, the team had fought well, bolstered by some fine individual performances.

In later years Tom may well have rued the lost opportunity of a win. New Zealand staggered along for the next 26 years before recording their first test victory.

In the meantime, the list of first milestones for Tom mounted. The following season, the West Indies dropped in for their first encounter with a New Zealand side, managing to squeeze in an appearance against a Wellington X1. The West Indies team included the legendary Learie Constantine, and while there were no runs for Tom, the match added to his ground-breaking captaincy. On the 1927 tour of England, he had also captained New Zealand in their first match against Ceylon (now Sri Lanka), in Colombo on their journey home.

The 1930-31 season was a dress-rehearsal for the England tour, though there were only the usual three first-class matches. Tom was still in good touch with the bat, averaging 45 in the Plunket Shield while leading Wellington to the title.

Tom was an automatic choice to skipper the 1931 touring team to England, but might not have been expecting his task to also include managerial duties. Lack of money again dictated team numbers being limited and Tom, always prepared to act in the best interests of the game, unconcernedly filled both positions.

When it came to extra duties, nothing perturbed him too much and before the tour he fulfilled another task, being co-opted on to the selection panel to help complete the team selection after some "certainties" had been named early. When Tom's reserve wicketkeeper duties are also considered, it is clear he was fully extended on tour.

The automatic choices to tour with Tom were Curly Page (Tom's vice-captain), Stewie Dempster, Jack Mills, Roger Blunt, Ken James and Bill Merritt, who had all toured in 1927, and Cyril Allcott, a left-arm spinner. Like Tom, Allcott had other duties – he looked after the tour finances.

Tom and the other selectors needed to name an additional six players. The skipper pushed hard for Ian Cromb after coming up against the Cantabrian during the Plunket Shield season. Tom, heading for a century, was beaten several times by Cromb, and was eventually lbw for

PRICE 6D.

SOUVENIR SCORING CARD

FOURTH TEST MATCH
(by Courtesy of the M.C.C.)

M.C.C. v New Zealand

Eden Park, Auckland

FEBRUARY 21-22-24, 1930

Hon. Sec. N.Z. Cricket Council:
W. H. Winsor

Umpires:
K. Cave and L. Coheroft

DEWAR'S WHISKY !

THE SPORTING SPIRIT

Sole Agents:
HANCOCK & CO. LTD.
AUCKLAND

The fourth test of the series in which New Zealand was granted official test match status.

LEFT: Opposing test captains in 1930 – Harold Gilligan of England and Tom.

101

91. Cromb got the nod. The other five places were taken by a couple of gifted youngsters, Giff Vivian and Lindsay Weir, a stroke player in Ron Talbot, and medium-fast bowlers Don Cleverley and Mal Matheson.

No sooner had the team been finalised than a national disaster nearly aborted the whole venture. On February 3, 1931, an earthquake, centred in Hawke's Bay, killed 256 people, creating fierce fires and destroying nearly all the stone and brick buildings of Napier. The fate of the tour hung in the balance and the Cricket Council released a statement signalling that the tour might have to be abandoned. A good part of the backing for the tour had been guaranteed by private individuals in the Hawke's Bay area (including Tom's father) and now some of them were forced to withdraw. But with the help of the Government, a national lottery was launched in a combined cricket and football deal, all motivated by a general desire that the tour should proceed. And so the team sailed for England at the end of March, a month-long journey on the New Zealand Shipping Company's new motor-liner, the Rangitata.

Eight decades later, it's difficult to comprehend the enormity of these tours. For some of the players it would be the trip of a lifetime as they were exposed to public attention like never before, had the chance to meet prominent people from royalty down, and experienced the culture of the Home Country.

The skipper contemplates the tour ahead. Tom relaxing on board the Rangitata en route to England.

An example of the interest in the tourists came at their welcoming British Sportsman's Club luncheon, presided over by Lord Harris. Tom sat at the top table with Lord Harris, three other Lords, three Knights, a Field Marshall and two Earls, plus his vice-captain, Curly Page. Scattered around the tables were William Wakefield (of rugby fame), Percy Chapman, Sir Malcolm Campbell, Harold Abrahams, Arthur Porritt and a host of other luminaries. As always, Tom took it all in his stride, replying to the toast in his deliberately underplayed down-to-earth fashion, helped by a few scribbled remarks on the back of his menu. He created rather a ripple when he explained the New Zealand Government had helped defray the tour expenses by running a lottery, an idea regarded by those assembled to be rather "progressive".

This was just the start. At a warm-up match against the Maori Club (if ever a name was a misnomer this was, with not a Maori in sight) at Worcester, with a bevy of photographers in attendance, Tom introduced every member of the team to the British public through the new-fangled medium of British Movietone News. Then when the New Zealanders travelled to Leyton for their opening first-class match, against Essex, a fleet of saloon cars was placed at their disposal by the Armstrong Siddeley Motor Company. Tom, as always, insisted on punctuality, and got the team away on time, only to have his plans foiled by the ineptitude of the drivers, who took them off on the wrong route and straight into a traffic-jam.

The match began late.

Some of the pressures may have placed his batting concentration under strain as the early part of the tour unfolded. For the first 11 games, he struggled to score runs, often getting to

Tom (with umbrella) inspecting the wicket before the start of play against Hampshire at Bournemouth. Also pictured, from left: Ian Cromb, umpires Frank Chester and Arthur Morton, Bill Merritt (obscured), Giff Vivian and Jack Kerr.

double figures but not carrying on. There was one notable exception – the MCC match (as described in chapter one), when a combination of special occasion plus need brought out the best in him.

You couldn't keep Tom down for long, and eventually against Minor Counties, five weeks after the start of the tour, he began a run of good scores. He may have been boosted by a surprise success at the bowling crease. He took six wickets in the match, bowling his famous "headers" – full tosses aimed at the body with a ring of fieldsmen spread far and wide on the leg side. These temptations proved too tasty for the batting side because four of his victims were cleaned bowled when he came around the wicket and straighted the ball on a turning pitch.

Tom was to finish top of the tour bowling averages with 15 wickets, and he always showed canniness at the bowling crease. Others had more faith in his bowling ability. When Tom returned to New Zealand, he was met by a customs officer, his old Auckland University club captain, who remarked: "Well Tom, I always had hopes of making a bowler out of you and now I see you've topped the averages." Tom replied: "Yes, that's when the skipper decided to take me off."

The editor of *Wisden* was more sceptical in his tour review, stating: "Lowry seldom exploited his weird bowling theories against the better batsmen."

Besides getting among the wickets against Minor Counties, Tom also scored a half-century. He then showed he was really coming right with 85 against Northants, the match preceding the first test.

RESPECTFULLY DEDICATED
TO THE NEW ZEALAND CRICKETERS
WHO PLAY ENGLAND AT
LORD'S TO-DAY.

THEY ARE THE BEST
FRIENDS WE (OR
ANYBODY ELSE)
COULD HAVE -

CAPTAIN & MANAGER

TOM
LOWRY
MAY
THE
BALL ALWAYS
BOUNCE
NICELY
FOR
YOU.

Best wishes for New Zealand on the eve of their biggest cricket challenge – the Lord's test.

There was a noticeable improvement in the defensive side of his batting. In *Archie's Last Stand*, Ian Cromb described how in the Middlesex match Tom's love of a challenge came to the fore: "Against Middlesex we lost four wickets quickly and I was preparing to go out to bat. Tom pushed me aside and went out to do battle against Gubby Allen, whom he regarded with a certain degree of disdain. In a hurry to get to the crease, Tom had forgotten to wear a box, and the first ball hit him where his protector should have been. In anger he threw his gear on the ground and rushed off past the startled old gentlemen in the Long Room and put on a large wicket-keeper's box. The next ball he received from Allen he played with his stomach, just like a tank, to the amusement of all those at Lord's."

Before the first test there were more social engagements. At the New Zealand Society annual dinner at the Savoy Hotel, attended by 287 guests, Tom was placed next to the special guest, Prince George (later Duke of Kent). On the menu was: Saddle of New Zealand lamb; New Zealand apples; and (with a nod to the touring skipper) Moawhango sauce served with asparagus (probably made with New Zealand butter). The Prince gave a splendid speech, hailing the quality of New Zealand's sportsmen and its farming production and in an acknowledgement to the scientific world, Lord Rutherford. Tom replied that anything his team might know about cricket had been learned from England and the fact they had been granted a test was an acknowledgement by the cricket authorities they had passed through the "knickerbockers stage".

The first test, at Lord's, was hailed as history-making. It was the first official test for New Zealand (later to be replaced by the retrospective recognition of the 1930 series). And what a crowd-pleaser it turned out to be, with 25,000 spectators present when Mills and Dempster opened on the first day. New Zealand competed strongly except for part of their first innings, when an excellent start was frittered away by the middle order. Tom's captaincy was criticised after England, still behind New Zealand's 224 at 190-7, allowed Les Ames and Gubby Allen batting at Nos 7 and 9, to score centuries on the second day. Tom had opened up with the leg-spinners Bill Merritt and Roger Blunt.

But in a match of changing fortunes, New Zealand struck back, scoring 469 in the second innings, with Dempster and Page getting hundreds and Blunt 96. Later, a typical skipper's knock by Tom held the innings together and avoided a collapse that would have allowed England time to win the match.

Tom was a frequent subject for the caricaturists.

Tom had pushed himself down the order after injuring his hand taking the catch that ended England's first innings. Ian Cromb, who rated Tom the second best bat (behind Dempster) on tour, in alluding to this innings, described Tom as a man of "infinite courage who would go in when the team was in a desperate position and stay there, getting runs until the danger had passed and a good total was in sight".

Tom declared, setting England 240 to win in 140 minutes, but Douglas Jardine never accepted the challenge. In the end England were forced to grimly fight out time with New Zealand picking up five wickets. It was clear that Tom was happy with the result. He fielded the last shot of the match and despite the protests of umpire Joe Hardstaff, walked off the field with the ball in his pocket. While Tom's tactics may have been misplaced on the second morning, Budge Hintz believed he had out-generalled Jardine in the match. The fact that Tom had been able to declare an innings closed against England at this stage of New Zealand's development as a cricket nation was clearly a moment of considerable (but quiet) pride for

Team photo before the start of play in The Oval test. Back row: Ron Talbot, Bill Merritt, Mal Matheson, Ian Cromb Ken James, Roger Blunt, Giff Vivian. Front row: Jack Mills, Curly Page, Tom, Cyril Allcott, Lindsay Weir.

the skipper.

As with the earlier tour match against MCC, the press lauded the "gallant" New Zealanders. The *Daily Mail* declared the test had fully proved the right of the young New Zealand players to take their places in the front line. The Governor-General, Lord Bledisloe, cabled Tom: "Heartiest congratulations on the team's fine achievement and splendid pluck in the test match. The Dominion is justifiably enthusiastic." This was followed by Prime Minister George Forbes, who wrote: "New Zealand warmly congratulates your team on its splendid performance in the test match, which worthily upheld the best tradition of British Cricket. We send cordial wishes for the remainder of the tour." Not only was there thunderous applause from back home, but in England, too, the clamour went up for a further test match to be played and a week later the England cricket authorities obliged by awarding two further tests.

All this kudos spurred Tom to a new level of consistency with the bat. He followed the test with 51 against Notts and then a fine double against Lancashire, 92 (scored at a run a minute) and 58 not out. He was run out for 89 against Combined Services and was finely tuned for the second test, at The Oval. His runs against Combined Services were made at better than a run a minute. Tom constantly took singles off the last ball of the over, but it eventually brought his downfall when he was run out.

Unfortunately for New Zealand, star batsman Stewie Dempster was sidelined with a muscular injury before this second test, and this was a crippling blow. New Zealand struggled to get into the match after England won the toss and Sutcliffe, Duleepsinhji and Hammond all posted centuries. Rain before the start of the second day freshened up the pitch for the England bowlers and Gubby Allen, bowling erratically but with considerable pace and fire, had taken 4-4 when Tom came to the crease. Budge Hintz wrote: "His side was faced with defeat, and yet Lowry batted as if victory were already in sight. His defence was magnificent, and never has that unbelievably powerful short-arm square cut been better employed. Finally a well-pitched leg-spinner saw him play a tentative shot and give an easy catch to Jardine at backward point. It was not his 62 runs that mattered; it was the manner in which he made them. This innings may not be given a place in the records of cricket, where so much depends on mere figures, but it will always remain in the memories of those who saw it as an exhibition of pluck and determination as inspiring as the game can provide."

Douglas Jardine described Tom's knock as the best innings seen at The Oval for many years because the wicket was so troublesome. New Zealand failed to save the follow-on and were bowled out again to allow England to win by an innings.

Still the runs kept coming for Tom. There was another 96 against Gloucestershire, when he hit nine fours during his 83-minute stay before being trapped in front. This was the prelude to the third test, a washed-out disappointment at Old Trafford in which there was only three hours' play.

Tom displaying some betting slips with Ian Cromb and Ron Talbot.

Tom struck his second century of the tour against Essex, scoring 129 with the century coming up in even time. This innings underlined his improved form – his previous 26 innings had produced an average of 45. Overall he finished fourth in the tour averages behind Dempster, Blunt and Mills, with 1290 runs at an average of 31.

It was a measure of Tom's mark on this tour that some critics said he would have been a certain choice as England captain had he been available. He was universally praised for his extensive knowledge of opposing batsmen's strengths and weaknesses, his speed in detecting vulnerabilities in the defence of those players he had not previously encountered, his skilful field placing and his masterly handling of his limited bowling resources. He became expert at nursing his quicker bowlers, never bowling them into the ground against batsmen who were set, but

Tom has some fun on a motorised bike at Sir Julien Cahn's residence.

keeping at least one of them ready and fresh to attack an incoming batsman. When it came to the spinners he would introduce the left-armer Allcott when Duleepsinhji came to the crease (Allcott got his wicket in the first two tests) and would use Page's off-spinners against the left-handers.

Former England captain Arthur Gilligan said of Tom at the end of the tour: "Tom Lowry made his mark here in 1927, when he captained the first New Zealand touring side, and he has added further honours to himself by his excellent captaincy in 1931. He is a great

Tom hits Derbyshire opening bowler Archie Slater aggressively off the back foot. He made a quick-fire 39 in a rain-affected draw. The wicketkeeper is Harry Elliott.

fighter and never admits defeat until the last ball is bowled. His personal charm made him very popular with everyone he met, and wherever the New Zealanders played one heard nothing but praise and pleasure for the sporting cricket they played."

Few New Zealand cricket tours have asked so much of one person, on and off the field, and received such an abundant return. Once Tom's early season batting staggers were over, he was consistently in the runs. He concentrated for hours as he unflinchingly fielded in the ever-demanding position of short leg, where he took many fine catches. Just to add to the burden, he would fill in behind the stumps for Ken James whenever the No 1 keeper needed a rest. Add the captaincy and then take into account the managerial duties and it becomes obvious that only someone with extremely broad shoulders and an even temperament could have carried out such a Herculean task.

Tom took it in his stride. He knew how to discard the minutiae. Scorer Bill Ferguson once saw him tear up communications from home exclaiming: "I came abroad to play cricket, not to write letters." Ferguson was one who was able to observe Tom at close quarters, finding a "quiet-spoken individual who could swear like a trooper if it suited him…but very easy to get along with."

Off the field, Tom received great help from Cyril Allcott, who looked after the finances. Later in the tour, Arthur Donnelly took over some of the managerial duties. His arrival in

RIGHT: The New Zealanders drew considerable coverage in the English newspapers.

NEW ZEALAND CRICKETERS

NORTHAMPTONSHIRE LOSE

VICTORY BY SIX WICKETS.

GOOD BATTING BY KERR.

LOWRY AGAIN BOWLS WELL.

By Telegraph—Press Association—Copyright.
(Special to N.Z. Press Association.)
PETERBOROUGH, June 23.

The New Zealand cricketers gained a meritorious victory over Northamptonshire by six wickets.

Bakewell and Woolley added 90 runs for the fourth wicket in the county's second innings, but the remaining bats... ...ing against Mer...

GREAT BOWLING

IN

THE TEST MATCH

Allen Takes Five for Fourteen

A CAPTAIN'S INNINGS BY LOWRY

New Zealand Forced to Follow-On

ENGLAND... 1st inns. 416 for 4 dec.
NEW ZEALAND ... 1st inns. 193
2nd inns. ... for 1

NEW ZEALAND AT SOUTHEND

ESSEX IN TROUBLE

Facing the huge total of 412 scored by New... ...aland, Essex, at Southend yesterday, were... ...out for 150 runs and, following on, lost... ...ykes's wicket for 53.

The New Zealand side revealed the real... ...th of their batting. Yesterday morning...

NEW ZEALANDERS

HAMPSHIRE SENT IN TO BAT

LOWRY JUSTIFIED.

In continuation of the Bournemouth... ...estival Hampshire yesterday met the New... ...Zealanders. The conditions were not so fav... ...urable for batsmen as in the match with... ...urrey. Rain had fallen in the early morn... ...ng, and with spells of sunshine the pitch... ...eemed to suit Vivian, the slow left-hand... ...owler, and, winning the toss, T. C. Lowry,... ...he New Zealanders' captain, adopted the... ...old course of sending Hampshire in first.

That it was a wise move was evident in... ...he course of the play before lunch, seeing... ...hat five batsmen were dismissed for the... ...neagre total of 67. Arnold was quickly sent... ...ack, and only Brown and Mead played with... ...ny confidence against a sound attack which... ...owry changed seven times in the first hour.... ...here was a breakdown in the weather early...

ENGLAND'S SLOW BUT SURE START IN THE TEST

SUTCLIFFE AND DULEEPSINHJI IN SECOND-WICKET STAND

LOWRY'S PROBLEM ON A DEAD PITCH

By HOWARD MARSHALL

BY WINNING the toss and scoring 312 for three wickets, England have started well against New Zealand in the second Test match, which began at the Oval yesterday.

In a sense the play was uneventful, though Sutcliffe and Duleepsinhji both made centuries on a wicket which gave no help to the bowlers.

Superficially it would appear that the batting was unenterprising, and it is true that Sutcliffe took four hours to make his runs, and that Hammond and Ames treated the bowling with exaggerated respect dur... ...the last half-hour.

There... ...Lowry, the New Zealand captain, ap...

NEW ZEALAND TEAM AT PORTSMOUTH

CAPTAIN'S INNINGS BY T. C. LOWRY

FROM OUR CRICKET CORRESPONDENT

The play in the match between the Combined Services and New Zealand at Portsmouth yesterday was most interesting, but if a definite result is to be obtained to-day someone will have to bowl unusually well. The New Zealand bat... ...men, having... ...coll... ...by... ...thin... ...Zeal... ...close... ...had... ...weat... ...ground... ...occas... music from the band of... ...Royal Marines, who may have a... ...professional, but certainly no more ch... ...ful, output than the bluejackets who... ...played on Wednesday.

New Zealand continued their innings... ...morning 294 runs behind on a pitch ap... ...ently unaffected by a heavy dew and still p... ...ing as quietly as ever. K. C. James, who... ...bat in any position from No. 1 to No. 11,... ...been sent in overnight to start the inn... ...with J. L. Kerr, and he at once settled do... ...to score runs, here, there, and everywh... ...The Combined Services started their bow... ...with Major Burrows and A. C. Gore, but it... ...not long before W. R. G. Melsome came o... ...place of Burrows. Kerr did not time the...

WELL DONE NEW ZEALAND!

By FRANK MITCHELL.

It is all in the luck of the game, of course, but many can-

COMBINED SERVICES OPEN WELL

Dempster and Test

NEW ZEALAND SKIPPER SHARES IN BOWLING

The New Zealand touring cricket team who visited Portsmouth to-day to meet the... ...on the Officers' Recre... ...in their side six players... ...Page, Blunt, Mills and... ...with the side who came... ...country in 1927... ...who were in the party... ...Merritt—were standing... ...med owing to his injured... ...r because he was taking...

Dempster is making such... ...ess towards recovery that... ...ugh to play in the next... ...a week to-day.

Services won the toss,... ...C. Wilkinson and Lieut.... ...ow out to open their...

that he was treated with the utmost respect by the batsmen, and he did not concede a run until Shaw on-drove the third ball of his fifth over for a couple.

He was not rested until the score was at 48, when he had put down eight overs (six maidens) nine runs, four of which came from one stroke, to leg, by Shaw. The half century was signalled after an hour's play. This was a very excellent start.

Vivian had relieved Allcott, and at 58 Matheson displaced Cromb. Both batsmen, although exercising a wise caution, picked out the right balls to hit, and Shaw was applauded for two fine on-drives to the boundary off Vivian.

First Faulty Stroke

NEW ZEALAND CRICKETERS

MATCH WITH LANCASHIRE

BATTING TRIUMPH ENJOYED.

WEIR SCORES FINE CENTURY.

LOWRY'S AGGRESSIVE DISPLAY.

By Telegraph—Press Association—Copyright.
(Special to N.Z. Press Association.)
(Received July 12, 5.5 p.m.)
LIVERPOOL, July 11.

The New Zealand cricketers enjoyed a batting triumph against Lancashire to-day. The weather was fine and the wicket perfect. The attendance was 8000. The teams were as follows:—

NEW ZEALAND.	LANCASHIRE.
Lowry.	Eckersley.
Page.	Hallows.
Weir.	

NEW ZEALAND'S GOOD SCORE

CENTURY BY T. C. LOWRY

The New Zealand team batted all day against Essex at Southend on Saturday, and at the close of play they had made 360 for the loss of eight wickets. T. C. Lowry, going in when four batsmen were out for 155, scored 129 runs in 2½ hours, and C. S. Dempster...

NEW ZEALAND'S GREAT HITTING

SEVENTY RUNS IN FORTY MINUTES

CRICKET

NEW ZEALAND TEAM AT NORWICH

DEMPSTER IN FORM

The New Zealand team began a two days' match against Norfolk at Norwich yesterday, and at the close of play Norfolk...

VIVIAN'S WICKETS.

NEW ZEALANDERS PLACED FOR A WIN AT SOUTHEND.

Weakened by the absence of Eastman, who had a swollen left hand, Essex, at Southend, yesterday, were badly outplayed and forced to follow-on 262 behind, and need 209 to save the innings defeat with one man out.

Apart from Pope, Nichols and Bray, Essex batted with little resolution. The swingers of Matheson caused an early breakdown in which three wickets fell for 40, and Vivian, bowling without relief for the rest of the innings, maintained, with Merritt, a skilful attack. Vivian sent down practically 29 overs and took four wickets for 25...

Tom showing his prowess on the golf course. Fellow smokers behind Tom's left shoulder, Roger Blunt (Blazer), Ron Talbot, Cyril Allcott, Ken James and Bill Merritt.

Illustrious names of cricket as the teams get together for the New Zealand versus England X1 game at Folkestone. Back row: Giff Vivian, Wally Hammond, Geoffrey Lowndes, Curly Page, Mal Matheson, Nawab of Pataudi, Les Ames, Ron Talbot, Maurice Allom, Ian Cromb, Frank Woolley, Jack Mills, Bill Merritt, Lindsay Weir, Frank Chester. Front row: Lord Tennyson (with microphone), Percy Chapman, Tom, Freddie Calthorpe, Stewie Dempster, Tich Freeman, Roger Blunt.

A farewell dinner for the tourists with cartoonist Tom Webster capturing the flavour of the occasion.

England before the first test coincided with Tom's change of fortune with the bat.

On his return to New Zealand at the end of the tour, Donnelly praised Tom's captaincy: "An outstanding feature of the tour from a playing point of view was the captaincy of Lowry. He covered the weakness of our bowling with great skill and displayed an almost supernatural ability in placing the field. Lowry is recognised in England as being a captain of the highest class, and it is not too much to say that if he were playing in England he would be captaining the side to tour Australia this season – he is ahead of any captain playing at Home today."

Donnelly may well have been biased in his comments, but no less an English cricket authority than Pelham Warner declared: "The New Zealander is the best skipper to tour England since the Australian Monty Noble in 1909."

Such was the interest in the 1931 tour that like the great All Black touring teams, the cricketers were welcomed home with a civic reception in Auckland. Dan Reese, the president of the New Zealand Cricket Council, delivered glowing words on Tom's captaincy which, he said, "placed him among the best in the world today. His performance has recalled the tactics of Noble, Trott and MacLaren. It may be that he is near the end of his cricket career – he has indicated that he will not be taking so active a part as formerly – but I'm sure that many will long cherish a vivid picture of his stalwart figure at the wicket. Tom Lowry emerges as one of the great figures in the game in this country."

Reese's remarks were greeted by thunderous applause, which was repeated again when Tom rose to reply to the various toasts. He said his men "feel quite embarrassed by the remarks that have been made and by the warmth of the welcome". Their proudest moment, he said, had been when they took the field against England at Lord's. "We had then played all the counties and felt we had at least a chance of winning. Realising that the good name of New Zealand was at stake, we got over the first nervousness and came out with honours even. The invitation of the MCC to a second test we regarded as an opportunity to put New Zealand on the cricket map."

A big turnout for the team's last match.

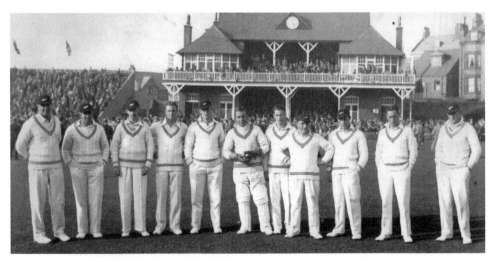

On board SS Ruahine bound for New Zealand after the 1931 tour.

Referring to the frequency of rain interruptions during the tour, Tom said: "If you have any trouble in Auckland with drought I shall be only too glad to get the team together and play a match," which was greeted by loud laughter. The welcome ended with three hearty cheers for Tom and his team.

If the 1927 tour was pioneering, 1931 established New Zealand as a genuine prospect for future cricket success. It revealed classy players in Stewie Dempster, Ken James and Bill Merritt, players capable of gracing any test-playing arena, while Tom's captaincy won acclaim as the best in the game at the time.

Furthermore, when the sun did shine, the spectators came out to watch. The gates were well up on 1927 (the tests helped) and receipts totalled £8000, not quite sufficient to meet the £9500 expenditure. But the Art Union lottery covered the loss as well as enabling the shareholders' capital to be returned, together with interest of six per cent.

Arthur Donnelly, in his capacity as New Zealand Cricket Council chairman, described the tour as "a magnificent success". It was a legacy of which Tom, in particular, could be justifiably proud.

9. Never Say Never

Tom, the oldest of the family, was the last to marry. He had watched his sisters wed his close friends Percy Chapman and Reg Bettington, and Ralph and Jim had married in the 1920s. There were compelling reasons for Tom's delay. First, his cricket career and touring had been all-consuming and this, combined with his daily farming, left time for little else. Then, when it came time to make up his mind, the country was in the throes of the 1930s depression. But he chose well and didn't have to go far to find the love of his life.

Margaret (Margot) Russell was the daughter of Gertrude (Williams) and Major General Sir Arthur (Guy) Russell of Tunanui, Hawke's Bay, the leader of the New Zealand Forces in World War I. At 12, Guy Russell moved from Hastings to Harrow and didn't return to New Zealand until he was 23. By World War I, he was acknowledged as a brilliant military man, masterminding, among other deeds, the evacuation of the Anzacs in the last 48 hours of Gallipoli.

Modest and unassuming, he went on to be a driving force behind the Returned Services Association in New Zealand, and moved to England for a period to set up the British Empire Servicemen's League. The Major-General was also something of a renaissance man – widely read, fluent in French, an enthusiastic cellist, an opera lover and a brilliant conversationalist. His grandchildren remember dinner occasions when he would stand up at the end of the meal and talk inspiringly and eloquently about some special person from his past – a friend, a leader, or a lowly, deceased soldier.

Margot was the youngest daughter in this family of three girls and two boys. She went to school at Woodford House and finished her education in Europe while her father was on his post-war assignment in England.

The Russells and the Lowrys were neighbours. Tunanui was about 10 miles up the road from Okawa, a sheep station settled in 1861, three years after Thomas Lowry moved on to Okawa. So the Russells and the Lowrys were lifelong friends and Tom and his siblings mixed with their Russell counterparts.

Tom's daughter, Carol, understood the Russells thought the Lowry boys, in their young adulthood, were a bit wild and needed to be treated with some wariness. On one occasion Tom turned up at Tunanui in the morning still wearing his patent leather shoes from a dance the previous night, and this was frowned upon. It emerged sometime later that the Russell parents had given an edict to their children: none should marry a Catholic, or a Lowry. The oldest son duly married a Catholic and Margot got hitched to Tom.

Based on their age difference of eight years, it's likely Tom and Margot had little to do with each other growing up. But they got to know each other much better when Tom, marshalling a mob of sheep down the road near Pukehaumoana, met Margot driving down the road to Hastings. They stopped for a chat and a cigarette and it picked up from there.

Tom with his brother-in-law, Andy Russell, and his father-in-law, Guy Russell.

Similar farming backgrounds were obvious reasons for Tom and Margot to get together, but Margot's ability with horses would have sharpened Tom's instincts that this was the woman for him. Margot was not only a fine horsewoman, riding hunts well into her 50s, but was also an astute judge of horse flesh and became Tom's partner and confidant in his long and distinguished association with the racing game.

Their marriage worked, according to daughter Carol, because while Tom was a "black and white" thinker, Margot was adept at "pointing out the grey bits". Others talked of her mellowing effect on Tom.

While they may have come from families not short of a bob or two, pecuniary matters caused a delay in their wedding plans. Their courtship was conducted in the midst of the depression, with devastating numbers of unemployed leading to hardship and often destitution. On top of that, the region was devastated by drought in 1930, followed by the 1931 Hawke's Bay earthquake.

These catastrophes were poignantly recorded in a diary kept by Guy Russell:

June 27, 1930: "No rain – outlook serious."

August 1: "Sheep very poor, am anxious."

August 8: "State of sheep and paddocks deplorable."

December 22: "Drafting lambs, 155 fats, expected 250."

February 3, 1931: "Earthquake. All chimneys damaged, work disorganised."

February 6: "Getting very dry."

July 22: "Feed and stock in deplorable state – feel puzzled and despondent."

Rain eventually started falling on July 24. The Tunanui accounts for the year 1930-31, according to Guy on September 17: "My annual accounts nearly ready and show a devastating loss."

Wedding day for Tom and Margot at Tunanui, 1933. Best man is New Zealand Cricket Council chairman Arthur Donnelly.

The following year was not much better and on January 8, 1932: "Expect to lose £1000 this year."

By 1933 things were starting to get better and Tom said: "Now we can get married." But reflecting the times, the wedding party that assembled at Tunanui was noticeably small when compared to the obvious lavishness of the Percy and Beet and the Reg and Marion weddings. Margot had just two young attendants and Tom's best man was Arthur Donnelly. A crown prosecutor and chairman of directors of the Bank of New Zealand, Donnelly had become a great friend of Tom's after winning his trust while chairman of the New Zealand Cricket Council. After appearing at the Imperial Cricket Conference in1931, Donnelly had become the de facto manager of Lowry's 1931 touring team.

After the marriage, Margot moved with Tom to the Pokaka property at Moawhango. The house they lived in was no more than a couple of nissan huts, and compared to what they had been used to at Okawa and Tunanui, was modest but workable. Margot adapted splendidly and always described her Taihape days as very happy ones.

Before long, they were full participants in the local community, helped immeasurably by having their woolshed double as a badminton court given over for the use of neighbours and friends.

It was clear from the end of the 1931 tour, and with Margot on the scene, that Tom's cricket would soon take second place to his changing priorities. He had also started to put on weight and had lost some of his agility in the field.

Tom's children settling down to life at Okawa. From left: Pat, Ann, Carol, Tom Junior.

He made himself unavailable to play for New Zealand during the first visit by a South African side, in 1931-32, but still captained Wellington to victory in the Plunket Shield competition.

In September 1932, the *New Zealand Herald* reported: "Word has been received in Wellington that TC Lowry, Wellington and New Zealand cricket captain, has decided to retire from active participation in cricket. It is stated that Lowry is unable to devote time to practise, a matter which would mean a good deal of travelling for him and without having this, he feels he would not be justified in carrying on with the game." The *Herald* went on to praise his career and leadership, regretting his withdrawal from the game, and adding "how greatly he was missed as New Zealand leader when the South Africans were here". As with so many retirements, this wasn't to be the end of the road for Tom's cricket because, first, he was talked into two more appearances for Wellington in the 1932-33 season and, much later, there was more cricket to come for New Zealand.

In the meantime, married life with Margot, starting a family (their first daughter, Ann, was born in 1934, Tom Junior followed in 1936, Pat in 1938 and Carol in 1943) and his farming-life commitments took over.

There were other matters to get in order. Tom was never one to be overly organised with his paperwork, and friends referred him to an accountant, Dick Sewell from Wanganui. Sewell had the redeeming feature of being a useful cricketer and subsequently was part of many teams playing friendlies at Okawa.

Before the 1931 tour to England, Tom delivered a battered old suitcase to Dick, saying: "Go through this and sort out this stuff." The suitcase revealed a potpourri of dog-eared invoices and an assortment of papers, with scrub-cutters due to be paid, accounts to be looked after and no little work required to get everything in order. On his return from England, Dick handed Tom everything he had done. Tom scanned the papers for about 60 seconds, then said: "We'd better have a drink."

Much of Tom's cricket was now for the Moawhango club in Taihape where, to be blunt, the standard was indifferent. In one match, the *Wanganui Chronicle* reported: "Lowry soon changed the state of the game by scoring 50 in about 40 minutes when he then decided to hit out, doubling his score in the next 20 minutes. Only the foresight of the opposing captain, Dr Sinclair, who stationed a man on a neighbouring hilltop, ensured the only ball was not lost." Given the standard, it was no surprise that the sociability of the cricket days was just as important as what happened on the field of play. Tom was certainly no wowser when it came to dispensing hospitality to Moawhango supporters. On one occasion, he was circling the boundary pouring whiskies when he met a local, Tom Whittle, who instantly had his glass three parts filled with whisky. When Tom picked up the water jug, Whittle muttered: "No water Tom, I find it gives me indigestion."

In early 1936, Tom consented to captain Rangitikei in a two-day match against Errol Holmes' MCC touring team, and in a Hawke Cup challenge match against Manawatu. Against the MCC, the home side was bowled out for 47, Tom getting just one, but he was the dominant Rangitikei player in an abortive challenge against Manawatu, showing what a fighter he was still by top-scoring in both innings (24 and 71 not out) as Rangitikei fell to an innings defeat.

He could still show, in no uncertain terms, how the game should be played. Tom captained the New Zealand Nomads against a weak Tokomaru side on Norman Cave's cricket ground and a team-mate, Douglas Cameron, scored 234 not out. When he reached his double-century, Tom sent a message out for Douglas to get himself out, whereupon Douglas took no notice and merely lifted the pace of his shotmaking. Tom turned to his team-mates and said: "I'll go in next and run the little so and so out." In went Tom and, hitting a ball towards deepish mid-off, he called for a quick run. Arriving at the bowler's end, he looked up to find Douglas still in his crease. After telling Douglas what he thought of him, Tom immediately declared the innings closed, much to Cameron's chagrin.

Arthur Donnelly, cricket benefactor and close friend of Tom.

With New Zealand's third tour of England beckoning, pressure mounted on Tom to go as player-manager. The costs of these tours of England were considerable. The 1927 and 1931 tours ran at considerable losses, and if Tom could double as a back-up to wicketkeeper Eric Tindill, then a worthwhile saving was possible. Tom agreed to go, based very much on the pleas of the New Zealand Cricket Council that it could find no-one else to do the manager's job. His decision was also eased by the fact that Margot would be joining him, a decision with bonus benefits because she graduated to a mother confessor role for some of the younger members of the side. Private backing was again needed to help finance the tour, and 14 guarantors, including Tom's father, TH, and Arthur Donnelly, fronted up to help make the tour possible.

The touring team appeared, on paper anyway, to promise plenty. It was captained by Curly Page, Tom's vice-captain from 1931, and included a future all-time great, Martin Donnelly, just 18, plus other batsmen Walter Hadlee, Merv Wallace, Bill Carson, Lindsay Weir, Jack Lamason and Eric Tindill (also the wicketkeeper), and bowlers Jack Cowie, Jack Dunning, Norm Gallichan and Alby Roberts. Giff Vivian and Sonny Moloney were the all-rounders. In fact, the team proved disappointing and it wasn't until the next tour of England, in 1949, that Hadlee's team, featuring the now-experienced Donnelly, Cowie and Wallace, performed so admirably and clearly showed the benefits of the 1937 experience. The '37 team, like that of 10 years previously, encountered an appalling English summer and the handicap of playing on wet wickets proved formidable.

From the outset, Tom sounded a word of warning that not too much should be expected from "a combination of amateur club cricketers". About this time there was a clamour for brighter batting and Tom, speaking at a welcome to the New Zealanders at the British Sportsman's Club luncheon, said: "We will try to play as brightly as we can, but we are not going to sacrifice any game to attain that end." Tom's method of speaking at these occasions was to jot down a few headings on the back of the menu and then, in a-matter-of-fact presentation, deliver what needed to be said. His speeches were never flowery, or those of a natural speechmaker, but they reflected his down-to-earth manner and were always sincere and well-meant.

At the Sportsman's club luncheon he spoke in front of New Zealand Prime Minister Michael Joseph Savage, in London for the Imperial Conference and the King's coronation, Jack Lovelock, fresh from his 1500m triumph at the 1936 Berlin Olympics, Doctor Arthur Porritt and a who's who of English cricket.

Within days of this function, Tom, Margot and Curly Page were off to Westminster Abbey for the coronation. The beautifully-embossed invitation had arrived.

Coronation of their Majesties King George V1 & Queen Elizabeth
By Command of The King
The Earl Marshall (Norfolk) is directed to invite Mr & Mrs T.C. Lowry to be present
at Abbey Church of Westminster 12 May 1937
This card must be shewn at the door

When the day arrived, panic stations set in after the invitations went down the laundry chute, and frantic efforts were needed to recover them (they've survived to this day without any noticeable damage other than a little ageing). There was also some good-natured banter among team members when Tom and Curly Page were sighted in the court regalia required for the coronation – knee breeches, buckled shoes, swords and tricorn hats. Photographs of the pair reveal countenances of some considerable sheepishness. The coronation was on the opening day of the second match of the tour, against MCC, and play was delayed to enable the players to watch the coronation procession.

Tom, starting to think about his match fitness, believed he was carrying a bit of weight and needed to fine down. He decided to play squash to quicken the process. In *Martin Donnelly* by Rod Nye, Donnelly describes how, in the first week of the tour, he was introduced to his

first game of squash by Tom.

"'You're the youngest. You can be my partner,' said Tom. I told him I'd never played before, but Tom proceeded to demonstrate the finer points of the game. This was all very well, but every time I played my shot and headed for the T, I collided with Tom's large frame. Still, it was great exercise, and despite the collisions there wasn't any serious damage." Tom did get fitter. He made his first appearances in the fifth and sixth matches and contributed to the tourists' first two wins. The first was a two-day game against Staffordshire, when he scored some runs (29 not out) in partnership with Giff Vivian, and the second was against his old University, Cambridge, when he displayed some behind-the-stumps trickery to pull off four stumpings, three from the leg-spinner Sonny Moloney.

Martin Donnelly, who was a close friend of Moloney, was delighted with his mate's success. "Tom Lowry wasn't the greatest wicketkeeper, but against Cambridge he and Sonny did some damage. Tom was rushing to the stumps, grabbing the ball before it reached them, throwing all three down. He combined wonderfully with Sonny, who earlier in his career was the type of bowler one would put on for a tempting over just before lunch: slow donkey-drops in the hope someone would hole out attempting a big hit."

Walter Hadlee in his autobiography also believed this game may have been where Tom acquired the nickname "Butch", with the stumps lying in the direction of slips or fine leg for each of the stumpings, indicating the ball had been taken in front of the stumps.

In *Kiwis Declare*, Jack Cowie told Nigel Smith that as a keeper, Lowry was a stopper. "This most dour and determined of bowlers tended to be less than amused by keepers who dropped catches. In one game there was a nick and Lowry dropped it. 'At the end of the over when we passed, he just said, "Do you think he hit that one?"' It is doubtful that Cowie burst out laughing."

Interviewed by the same author, Eric Tindill remembered Tom as "merely stooping behind the stumps rather than getting down on his haunches in the approved manner". While there were some understandable reservations about Tom's ability behind the stumps (after all he was in his 40th year), it should be also said that Tindill's hands suffered from the arduous tour itinerary and Tom was forced to play a little more than he wished or than his waning powers as a wicketkeeper justified.

Donnelly also remembered Tom's captaincy skills from behind the stumps in the Staffordshire match. "Norm Gallichan was bowling left-arm spin and I was fielding at extra cover. As we crossed over between overs, Tom said to me: 'Keep your eyes on me. When you get out there I want to shift you a few yards. Watch out because you'll get one in the midriff.' Inconspicuously Tom shifted me three to four yards, more towards cover. First ball next Gallichan over, I had the catch. I talked to Tom about this field placing skill and he gave the credit for whatever he'd picked up to his old Somerset captain, John Daniell. Whoever was bowling you always had the feeling Tom would find a way of getting the batsman out."

The question of back-up captaincy on the tour was contentious, with vice-captain Giff Vivian often overlooked if Curly Page was standing down and Tom was playing. Tom merely assumed what he regarded was his rightful position. Vivian and Tom has been good friends

LEFT: With Margot as they prepare to leave for the King's coronation in 1937.

Giff Vivian, the vice-captain on the 1937 tour, found Tom often undermined his authority.

on the 1931 tour, when the 18-year-old Vivian had been taken under Tom's wing and nurtured into a fine future all-rounder. In 1937, he was still only 24, but despite his youthfulness could have expected, as the tour vice-captain, a fair degree of sway when it came to picking teams and also to take over as captain if Page wasn't playing. This didn't happen. Tom and Page, leaving it until the last minute, would confer on team selection, sometimes omitting players for several games for no apparent reason. Vivian became very frustrated by this state of affairs and according to *Merv Wallace: A Cricket Master,* confronted Tom over the matter. But not much changed.

There was potential for more controversy when the first test loomed. Tom had run into some serious form, with reports describing his batting as "back to his best". Against Lancashire, he top-scored in the first innings with a belligerent 49, batting for 95 minutes in a chanceless display. New Zealand were beaten by an innings, but Tom was then included in the next match, against Nottinghamshire, when he again took centre stage, scoring 121. His first 50 included 10 fours and his century 18 fours and a six. The innings was described as "a grand exhibition of clean hitting".

"A magnificent display of monopolistic batting, a giant's innings from a giant of a man," reported the *Nottingham Journal.* The crowd, it said, had enjoyed his "stentorian calling, delivered with imperious command".

When the New Zealanders reached London for the Lord's test, the headlines were asking: "Will the New Zealand Manager Play?" Donnelly had lost form, and Vivian, Wallace and Roberts were

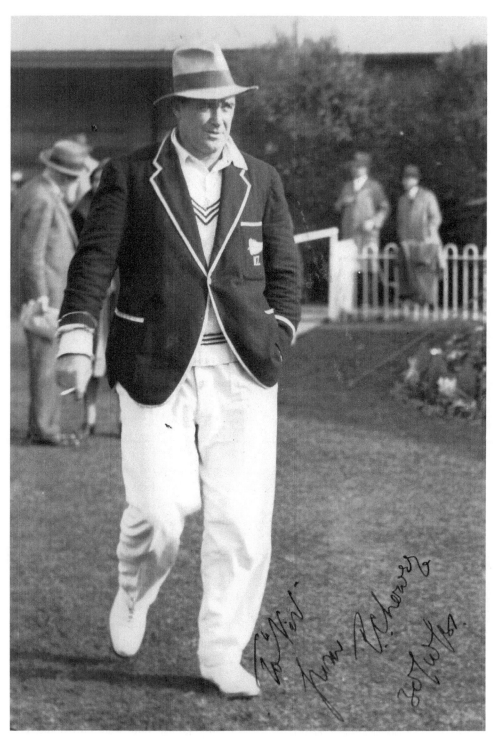

Tom was manager and the pseudo vice-captain of the 1937 team.

Jack Cowie, the outstanding bowler in the 1937 touring team.

under injury clouds. But one critic wrote: "The Dominion cricket world would be shocked if Lowry was included to the detriment of at least one left-arm bowler if Vivian is unable to take the field."

Tom himself was relaxed about it all and was keen to give the opportunity to a younger man. He was also suffering somewhat from bruising and soreness. The flurry of speculation didn't last. Vivian, Wallace and Roberts all passed fitness tests, Donnelly also played, scoring a duck in the first innings and being relegated to No 9 in the second. New Zealand drew the match.

Donnelly's first innings duck was his third in succession, but after the test he started to come right. In the Yorkshire match, before the second test, he scored a blistering 97, when to save the game circumspection appeared to be required. He was bowled playing a premeditated hook shot to a full-length ball from Bill Bowes. Donnelly left the field to a silent crowd that had witnessed his unnecessary recklessness. The manager was even more pointed. Tom told Donnelly: "I ought to take all three stumps and you'd know what I'd do with them." The tourists were heavily beaten in the second test and the third test was drawn after rain prevented any chance of a result.

Tom continued to play when required. In all, he made 12 first-class appearances on tour, as well as turning out in a number of two-day matches. At times his body suffered the aches and pains of a near-40-year-old playing at the top level. He scored 409 first-class runs at an average of 27, as well as contributing as a wicketkeeper.

Unfortunately, another wet summer contributed to a disappointing overall team performance. New Zealand lost seven county games and won only four. The batsmen lacked consistency and there was no opening bowler to back up the superb Jack Cowie, although Jack Dunning was a workhorse and performed well. Donnelly, with his elegant batsmanship, would go on to charm English cricket followers after World War II, and score a memorable double-century in the Lord's test on the 1949 tour of England.

There was never any doubt as to who was in charge on the 1937 tour. Tom, as he had done in 1927 and 1931, orchestrated the show from the start.

He was clearly an eminent figure among the English cricket establishment. Everyone knew and liked him, and this led to positive responses from whatever request came from the team. Not that he was over-zealous in pursuing every sundry invitation. Merv Wallace remembered sitting next to him when they were playing against Staffordshire. Lowry pulled a letter from his pocket. "It was apparently from the Royal Worcester Company, offering each of us a jug. 'Who wants a jug?' Tom said rather disdainfully. He was a wealthy man and perhaps didn't realise that a Royal Worcester jug would be quite an acquisition for some of the players."

Tom wasted little time on the written word. It was said that he wrote only one official letter on the tour, preferring word of mouth and his own sincerely delivered thanks when required. When it came to the press, he wasted few words, saying he needed his thoughts for his speeches. And like the Staffordshire story, he binned many of the invitation requests as unnecessary for the team.

Yet, when he felt the team would benefit from an experience, he would pull out all stops to make it happen. While he, Margot and Curly Page had ringside seats for the King's coronation, he was insistent that the players should have suitable places to watch the procession. All the players were up at five in the morning to get to their positions. Later, he arranged for the team to visit centre court at Wimbledon to watch the American, Don Budge, on his way to winning the singles title.

In a tour of on-field disappointments, he suffered his frustrations with the team. On a bad day, he would exclaim: "I've got a team of shepherds back home who could do better than this."

Merv Wallace said these homilies were always delivered in a humorous way and never offensively. After one of the team's early losses, he organised a net practice and made some very telling comments. "All I want you bloody batsman to do," he growled, "is play down the wicket where you last saw the ball." On another occasion, exasperated after another poor effort, he turned to Jack Cowie and asked: "Jack, what the hell's wrong with our batsmen?" Cowie thought for a moment, obviously not wanting to let his mates down, and after serious consideration, replied: "Well Tom, I don't think there's a great deal wrong with them, except we run out of them too quickly."

While the team knew Tom was in charge, compared to modern curfews and mollycoddling, he oversaw operations with a light touch. Many of the players liked a drink after play, and most were smokers, as was the custom of the time. There were no curfews. As far as Tom was concerned, players were expected to front up in a fit condition for play the next day.

During the three-match stop-off in Australia on the way home, Tom played his last first-class match. This was against Victoria at the Melbourne Cricket Ground, where he captained and kept wicket. There was no final triumph. He batted No 10 in both innings, being left not out in the second, and picked up a catch in each Victorian innings. The home side won by five wickets.

So ended his first-class career: 9421 runs at 31.19 (18 centuries); 49 wickets at 27.00; and 101 wicket-keeping dismissals, 52 caught and 49 stumped.

Tom gradually phased himself out of involvement with top-level cricket after this tour, though he was the sole New Zealand selector during the 1938-39 season (he had previously helped select the national team that, under Ian Cromb's captaincy, played the MCC in 1935-36).

His selection duties in 1938-39 were not onerous because New Zealand played just one match, a rain-affected international against Sir Julien Cahn's team in Wellington. Tom did, however, make one important decision. He chose fast bowler Tom Pritchard, the only time Pritchard was to represent New Zealand. Pritchard, an inexplicable omission from the 1937 team to Britain, settled in England after the war, playing for Warwickshire for a decade, so never represented New Zealand again.

10. The Racing Game

To use a well-worn sports cliché, Tom's life was very much a game of two halves. The first was dominated by his love of cricket and his impact on the game. The second was tied to horses and in particular their ownership, breeding and racing.

This passion for racing didn't happen by chance. His father, TH, learned much about its intricacies during his school years and time spent later in England. TH, in turn had been lured by its attractions through the interest of his father, Thomas.

In Thomas' days, during the second half of the 19th century, the sheep stations often held race meetings after the shearing season had ended. The shearers themselves were frequently the owners of good racehorses and with shearing lasting a number of weeks, the stations needed to provide good quality feed in the "night" paddocks. Okawa had a reputation for supplying the best. Thomas had no great knowledge of horses, but was very keen and spent a lot of money on developing his hobby. However, the extensive racing history retained by the Lowry family does not describe his purchases as thoroughbreds.

The early Hawke's Bay run-holders became New Zealand pioneers in setting up relatively large-scale breeding establishments. TH was certainly part of this, but was by no means the first. Others included the Ormonds at Karamu, Allan McLean (Tukituki), Sir William Russell (Flaxmere), George Donnelly (Crissoge), William Douglas (Te Mahanga), William Rathbone (Waipawa), W Broughton (Nga Puka) and Spencer Gollan (Mangatarata).

The Watt family, which, of course, TH married into, was also prominent, with James Watt later becoming the first president of the Auckland Racing Club (but not the same James Watt mistakenly described in New Zealand racing histories as the importer of Figaro, the first thoroughbred, and later sire, landed in New Zealand). His son Eddie, like TH, raced numerous horses in the early 1900s, and imported the well-bred English sire All Black, before moving to Australia to become a leading owner. Being in Australia didn't stop Eddie continuing his close association with the Lowrys, often as a visitor to the Trentham yearling sales where, on one occasion, he was facetiously accused of "stealing" one of TH's drafts for a bargain. It went on to win 16 races.

Once TH became committed to racing and breeding, he steadily built his reputation. In 1894 he won the Hawke's Bay Steeplechase with Gondolier, in 1904 the Hawke's Bay Cup with Madrigal and in 1906 the New Zealand Cup with Downfall. Nevertheless, this growing status was essentially based on his success in jumping and "bracelet" races (where the owner won a bracelet).

The Lowry name really became synonymous with racing in 1906, when TH engaged Fred Davis, a former Auckland jockey and part-time trainer, as his private trainer. This decision had the potential to fuel some family tensions. Davis had previously been Eddie Watt's stable horseman and now he moved to Watt's brother-in-law's property, together with a Finland gelding which Eddie had sold to Davis for £50. This Davis now off-loaded to TH for £150, a tidy profit but, at that stage, there was no prescient knowledge of what the gelding would achieve. The transaction, though, set TH and Davis on the path to racing fame (and some fortune).

The big black gelding that Fred Davis sold to TH was Bobrikoff, and while both undoubtedly recognised his potential, there were a couple of flaws that may have signalled likely impediments to major success. One was a suspect off-foreleg joint and the other a troublesome muscular ailment. The muscular trouble remained throughout his racing career. The answer to this problem was that TH and Davis set up a training stable at Paraeti, a beautiful little bay on the beach (later to disappear as a result of the Hawke's Bay earthquake), which enabled Bobrikoff and other stable-mates to swim in the salt water and ease what was suspected in Bobrikoff's case to be muscular rheumatism, and keep him racing.

The results were spectacular. From a three-year-old to a nine-year-old, Bobrikoff had 52 starts, and won 24 races over distances varying from five furlongs to two miles. This was all under the handicap of big weights and giving his opposition huge starts because of the time it took to warm up with his action.

An example of this was in the 1912 Auckland Cup, well described by John Costello in *Tapestry of Turf:* "Slow out of the stalls, Bobrikoff was obviously sore and got further and further behind the field, so much so that the crowd was calling on jockey Fred Jones to pull the old champion up as he passed the stands with a round to go. But Jones and Bobrikoff had other ideas. Going along the back, Bobrikoff was warming to his work and lengthening stride. Around the top bend he began to loop the field and in the home stretch, where the lightly-weighted roan mare La Reina appeared to be out on her own, Bobrikoff inexorably gathered her in and downed her by a neck." Jockey Fred Jones maintained Bobrikoff was the greatest galloper he ever rode.

Meanwhile, Fred Davis had made a second smart purchase for £30, a chestnut colt named Balboa, which again he on-sold to TH for another nice profit. TH's racing ownership dominance was just beginning. Balboa proceeded to win the Auckland Cup in 1915 and on the same day the Lowry stable raised the attention of the punters with Tete-a-Tete winning the Railway Handicap and Bjorneborg winning the Nursery Handicap. On the second day of the carnival, TH made a telling racing statement. In the Islington Plate, his filly, Desert Gold, trounced two impressive rivals. By the time the Christmas-New Year carnival was completed, Desert Gold had also won the Great Northern Derby and Royal Stakes, eclipsing Balboa's Auckland Cup triumph and becoming the glamour horse of the meet.

At this same Auckland Cup week, TH, with Balboa, Desert Gold, Finmark, Egypt, Bjorneborg, Tete-a-Tete and Bobrikoff, collected stakes in 13 out of 32 races over the four days of the carnival. The Lowry racing colours of gold jacket, navy sash and gold cap were now truly at the forefront of New Zealand racing.

Bobrikoff may have been a star, but Desert Gold was a champion. Bred at Okawa in 1912 by All Black out of Aurarius, Desert Gold is still regarded as among the very greatest of New Zealand thoroughbreds. Known variously as the "The Queen of the New Zealand Turf", "The World War One Glamour Girl", and "Australian Heroine", Desert Gold had it all – speed and an in-built fortitude that enabled her to hold out against the toughest challengers.

As a three-year-old, she was invincible, winning all 14 starts, a record not beaten until Mainbrace won 15 as a three-year-old in the 1950-51 season. Desert Gold then won her first four starts as a four-year-old and, when added to with her last-start win as a two-year-old, had built a winning sequence of 19. This record was eventually equalled by Desert Gold's great rival, Gloaming, and nearly a century later, the pair's record still stands.

Some of Desert Gold's wins as a three-year-old were staggering. She won the Great Northern Oaks by an official 150 yards and the inaugural Great Northern Ledger by 50 yards. As a five-year-old, she raced in Australia, winning two of her first three starts, the second in the Governor's Plate at Flemington to huge acclaim after TH announced that the mare's entire Australian stake earnings would go to the Patriotic Fund. A photograph of her head appeared on a cigarette packet that bore her name.

There followed two more wins in Sydney – the Autumn Stakes and All Aged Stakes. At Randwick, TH went to the Returned Soldiers Stand and gave 40 or 50 of them a fiver ($525 in today's terms) each and told them to put it on the mare. Of course, Desert Gold won. In *Galloping Greats*, Desert Gold's old apprentice jockey, Tim Williams, quoted 50 years later, said: "There was never a horse the public loved more." In 1918, Desert Gold had the rare honour for a mare of starting top weight in the Melbourne Cup, with 9st 6lb, but the cup that year was won by Night Watch, carrying just 6st 9lb, and Desert Gold was eighth.

The Melbourne Cup meet was the forerunner to a series of clashes against the next great New Zealand champion, the Australian-bred Gloaming. This was virtually a "three-match series" on the Taranaki circuit in the summer of 1919. Desert Gold won the first, at New Plymouth, Gloaming reversed the order at Egmont and the clincher took place at Hawera. Both horses had had to overcome difficulties in the first two races – Gloaming being caught in the starter tape at New Plymouth and in the second Desert Gold had to hurdle stablemate Croesus when the horse fell in front of her on the top turn. At Hawera, the lead swapped twice before Gloaming got home by two lengths, a signal for the changing of the guard.

Desert Gold may have eventually been eclipsed by her younger rival, but she finished with a stunning record: 59 starts, 36 wins, 13 seconds and 4 thirds. Through 1916, 1917 and 1918, TH was the top New Zealand-owning stakes winner, helped immeasurably by the efforts of Desert Gold, but backed by a stable of other top-performing horses, including Bobrikoff, Estland, Finmark and Balboa. Desert Gold's stake earnings of £17,224 (equal to about $1.8 million today) in 1918 were not surpassed for 30 years. The Lowry name was now indelibly linked with the best in New Zealand racing.

Tom's elevation into the racing game was almost preordained – it was as natural as his cricket development had been years earlier. His father was a cricket and racing man, and Tom instinctively followed the same path. He went to the races with his father and TH passed on what he knew. So when Tom settled down to farm at Moawhango, TH gave him two mares, including Sudan, which Tom raced during World War II. Aden from Sudan won the Wellesley Stakes. Tom took to racing with great enthusiasm, reverting to his inbuilt instinct for concentrating very intensely on whatever he decided to take up. He was never afraid to improvise and experiment. Tom Junior remembers his father teaching Desert Fox to become used to noise by kicking a kerosene tin in front of him as he led the horse around. Tom would use his immense, tractor-like strength to pull the horse along in the process of taming him.

The most expensive stallion imported to New Zealand to that time, Faux Tirage.

Tom moved to Okawa on TH's death in 1944, when the basic infrastructure for horses was still in place. Sam Brooks stayed on as the groom and Tom's keenness and dedication to the industry became entrenched.

At his death, TH owned Lambourn (who won the Wellington Cup the following year), and although he was sold, an arrangement allowed Tom to repurchase the entire once his racing career had ended. Lambourn was to sire some winners, but Tom let him go after an opportunity came to make the most significant purchase of his career, the English-bred stallion Faux Tirage.

The staggering sum of £25,000 (about $12 million today) paid for Faux Tirage almost certainly made it the most expensive stallion ever brought to New Zealand to that time. It was the same cost as the newly-built home at Okawa. An Englishman, Brigadier Scott, who worked for the British Breeders' Association and had a great knowledge of horses, had found Faux Tirage for Tom (as well as Northern Dancer for EP Taylor and Oncidium and Agricola for the Williams family).

Initially, Faux Tirage was considered to have stamina limitations and the brilliance of his early progeny when he headed the winning two-year-old lists with his first three crops seemed to confirm the belief, but such a suggestion was well put to rest when Straight Draw won the 1957 Melbourne Cup. Faux Tirage produced more than 30 stakes race-winners, including: Straight Draw; Knave (The AJC Epsom Handicap); Rover, a dual St Leger winner and top New Zealand three-year-old of his year in the Lowry colours; the dual Oaks and Auckland

Cup winner Froth; Hot Drop, another dual St Leger winner and top two-year-old of his year; and dozens of others, including Game, Baraboo, Rover, Gymkhana and Ma Cherie.

Tom's sister-in-law Edna (married to Jim) had bred Froth with great success after unusual circumstances, as recalled by Tom Junior. "Jim was a great party-goer and character, and went off to the Trentham yearling sales as usual, despite the birth of their first baby. In a fit of guilt, Jim bought a yearling filly and gave it to Edna. The filly won several races but, trained by an old drinking mate of Jim's, she fell away to nothing and was rescued by another friend. My father had his new expensive stallion and promised Edna a free service to Faux Tirage if she led the mare down to the stallion on foot the four miles across the paddocks. The result was Froth, who won the Oaks, the Auckland Cup, and later became Broodmare of the Year."

When Sir Patrick Hogan was just a lad of 18, he was staying with his aunt at Havelock North and said to her that he would love to visit "Mr Lowry's Okawa property" and see the famous Faux Tirage. Young Patrick, feeling somewhat nervous, duly drove out in his newly-acquired Vanguard, expecting to see the stallion out in his paddock with his rug on and with no thoughts of meeting Tom. Instead, Tom himself appeared and paraded Faux Tirage, beautifully groomed, on the Okawa lawns. After his inspection and a good chat, he was invited inside to share a soft drink. Today, Sir Patrick says it was a huge lesson and an insight into public relations and something he not only never forgot but consistently tried to live by during his long career running a thoroughbred stud.

Tom never forgot the meeting either. At the Trentham yearling sales, he would always go up to Patrick, pat him on the back and compliment him on the fine draft of yearlings he had paraded.

Faux Tirage, meanwhile, was the champion New Zealand and Australasian sire of 1958, the leading New Zealand sire of two-year-olds in 1954-55-56 and 1963, and achieved eminence as a sire of brood mares. Interestingly, given the early doubts, it was the versatility of Faux Tirage sires that established his name: brilliant sprinters; tough, game stayers; and reliable jumpers. Most of them could handle any type of footing. Faux Tirage spent his retirement years in the paddocks at Okawa and Tom Junior can still remember his father's tears when he died in January 1970.

Following Faux Tirage's retirement, Wyandank was Okawa's next importation, but was only moderately successful before being replaced by an American, Bourbon Prince, another expensive buy. Bourbon Prince's first crop showed speed, which led to them being treated as early comers when they needed time. He did not sustain his early success and was exported to Japan at considerable financial loss. By this time, his sons, Tom Junior and Pat, were having more influence and Pat, in particular, was instrumental in Tom purchasing Reindeer.

Tom said: "I'm too old to have this horse." But the boys convinced him he was never too old and to go ahead and buy Reindeer after he had stood for a season in the United Kingdom. Reindeer produced some early place-getters in the Melbourne Cup, but Tom Junior later said that "while he was a lovely horse, he wasn't a great sire".

There is no question that under Tom's guidance Okawa became one of the great thoroughbred nurseries of the southern hemisphere. There was blood of consistent quality in the stallions, and he had shares in others just as good (Oncidium and Agricola), plus a group of 50-odd brood mares with equally impeccable backgrounds.

A typical scene at Okawa – foals and mares grazing.

Sir Patrick Hogan observed that it should never be forgotten that Tom had to labour under the handicap of mixed farming, where the sheep and cattle were every bit as important as the stud aspect, a state of affairs that eventually changed with the likes of Hogan's Cambridge stud.

If the stud part of his business was hugely rewarding, Tom also had time to bask in the glory of having successful horses race in his own colours, or those of his and Margot's. There were few finer than Game, raced jointly by Tom and Margot. The magnificent black gelding won 26 races and was noted for his great courage. Consequently Game became one of the most loved racehorses in the country. It wasn't until he became a five-year-old that he started to really live up to his name. Before that, Tom had thought of him as only average. But Bob Quinlivan, his trainer, had found him "a quiet and wonderfully intelligent animal" and was instrumental in nursing Game through his successful career, always with the knowledge that the gelding wasn't completely sound.

Not everyone was impressed. Top jockey Grenville Hughes disparagingly described Game as "w-e-a-k, not game" when he rode Game as a three-year-old. But Quinlivan helped turn Game around and as a six-year-old he was unplaced only three times in 14 starts. Then when Game was a top weight-for-age seven-year-old, Hughes came back to ride him and repudiated his earlier statement. "Game," said Hughes, "was a real gentleman, with a wonderful personality, a wonderful temperament and wonderful will to win."

There were other fine performers, such as the Faux Tirage progeny of Rover and Humber. Then there was Super Snipe (Tom's preferred mode of transport), and Key, who won 19 races as a three-year-old and was totally dominant.

At the end of Tom's career, there was great satisfaction in the performances of Mop, the 1976 Marlboro filly of the year.

During his life, Tom left almost nothing in written form. There were no letters and his speeches were given off the back of an envelope. But what does survive is his written acceptance speech for the Mop award, made more poignant by the fact that because of poor

Tom during his racing and cricket administration phase.

Margot Lowry, an accomplished horsewoman, on Jungle.

health he was able to complete only part of the speech when he stood up to deliver it at the dinner in Hastings.

"This is, of course, a happy occasion to win the award with such good fillies about as Tudor Light, Mer'cler and Entice. We have beaten Tudor Light the only time we have met and Entice has beaten us twice, only to fall by the wayside at the end of the season, which was bad luck for David Geor.

"I think the competition is very fair, starting in Hawke's Bay in September and continuing till April, with more points for longer races. I don't see any point in altering the conditions of the award.

"In the South Island, they have their filly of the year competition too – not such good stakes, but better than hack races. I had an inquiry to lease some fillies to run in those races down south. The inquirer thought the races were well worthwhile.

"The purpose of the Marlboro competition is to encourage breeders to keep some of their best fillies. Whether this is working out I don't know, but certainly the better stakes must help.

"My filly, Mop, had an accident. She fell off a bridge and cut a patch of skin off her coronet and the blemish prevented her from going to the sales. It was not serious, but unsightly. So that is how I came by Mop. On cup day in Brisbane last week, there was a two-year-old race of a mile called the Marlboro Stakes of $30,000. The president told us that Godfrey Phillips had supplied the whole stake, plus a very large cup. That might be too much money for New Zealand, but still, it is something to set your sights on.

"Sir Charles Kingsford Smith, when leaving New Zealand in Southern Cross, thanked the gathering for their kindness and ended his remarks with the sensible observation that a few bob would be very handy. That's what I feel about the $5000 prize that Mop has won, the $1000 for the trainer and the $500 breeders' premium.

"Finally I want to say how much I appreciate the work of Keith Couper. It was his skill that made Mop what she is tonight."

Running his enterprise at Okawa, Tom could be tough on his staff. He most certainly didn't suffer fools gladly and his old cricket insistence on punctuality never left him. If a shepherd was not on time for the vehicle heading to a sale, Tom would depart without him, relying on his own knowledge to do the buying.

One time he sacked the entire team. On another occasion the head groom, Eddie Lowry (no relation to Tom), was in the firing line. This was after a vet had worked diligently all day to save an ailing horse. At the end of the day, Margot decided to let the horse out into a paddock and Eddie, not happy with the subsequent turn of events, suggested Margot should stick to the kitchen. Tom, on hearing of this, immediately requested Eddie apologise. Explaining to Tom that his wife had made the wrong decision and that he couldn't apologise, Eddie was sacked on the spot, only to be reinstated the next morning.

Eddie Lowry had been a great catch for the Lowry stud. Previously an apprentice with the Ted Winsloe stables at Gore, Eddie was the country's leading trainer and immediately struck a rapport with Tom at his interview. After some discussion, Tom said: "So can you start now?" Eddie's reply impressed Tom: "I need to go back to Gore and tell Mr Winsloe why I'm leaving." The conversation on his employment had covered a lot of ground and Eddie said: "I think we need to get some of this down on paper. What happens if you want to get rid of me after six months?" Tom said: "I do business with a handshake." Eddie shifted north, never forgetting that it had been 28 degrees in the shade when he arrived for his interview. He stayed for 30 years, which covered Tom's remaining years and then some with Tom Junior.

Tom was never a major racehorse punter, although he loved a bet on anything. Eddie Lowry remembers his constant need to bet on a rugby, cricket or golf match, even down to a lowly table tennis contest at Okawa. The bets were invariably for a packet of cigarettes. Eddie Lowry always believed he came off second-best in these contests, even when he bet correctly, because Tom would duly pass over his lethal Pall Mall Plain variety (these had replaced his old favourites, Capstan Plain, which lost favour in 1971 after a table of tar and nicotine contents of cigarettes was published and found that, by some margin, Capstan had the highest of both). Because of his distaste for them, Eddie would end up handing most of them back.

But Eddie said the over-riding impression of Tom and Margot and their race winnings was of their generosity to other people. Tom would take around trays of peaches, boxes of chocolates or cigarettes to those he felt needed a boost while Margot, who only ever backed group one winners with a five bob each way bet, would buy roses to plant for neighbours and friends.

Tom undoubtedly had a great eye for horse flesh. Son Pat and his wife Jane were having dinner with legendary trainer Tommy Smith in Sydney once and Tommy said: "Pat, have either you or Tom Junior got your father's eye for a horse?" Not only had Smith seen Tom in action at the big sales, but the respect they had for each other resulted in the two racing a number of horses in partnership. Eddie Lowry said he always marvelled at his boss's perception and the fact that he didn't mind his horses being small.

Above all, Tom's competitive streak from his cricket days never left him and he loved winning.

But he was never over-commercialised. While he had an inbuilt caution based on his debt-ridden days at Taihape during the depression, he would always have half a dozen horses in work at any one time and would use three or four runners at local meetings. And he would place horses in a number of Hastings stables as he tried to buck the trend of trainers being forced to move to the bigger racing centres. He would usually keep one or two good fillies a year, but never minded giving them away.

In his later years, he would present one or two fillies a year to each of his children (strongly encouraged by Margot), the proceeds of which enabled them to take care of Margot in later life. There was another reason for this – the avoidance of death duties – and racing horses in partnership, as they did, enabled this to happen.

Back in 1948, Tom took on a role that was to have longstanding significance for the racing industry. He was a driving force behind the formation of the New Zealand Thoroughbred Breeders' Association. Unhappy with their place in the National Alliance of Owners, Trainers and Breeders, about 40 prominent breeders got together, led by Ken Austin, Alister Williams and Tom, and formed an association along the lines of the British Thoroughbred Breeders' Association. The new association aimed to "encourage, promote, advance generally and ensure co-operative efforts in all matters pertaining to the production and improvement of the thoroughbred horse and to the interest of the thoroughbred breeders".

The inaugural president was Ken Austin, but in the year of formation he was replaced by Tom, who led the association for the next 17 years.

Stan McEwan, doyen of racing writers, wrote: "TC Lowry developed the association's policy and guided its affairs with a dignity which gained it prestige and with wisdom and strength which commanded respect, from the highest administrative circles in New Zealand and Australia. The industry will remain in his debt." A later president said of Tom and the association that "he stood like a rock while we built it up around him".

The new association had much work to do and Tom led the way in many vital areas.

The first was building a lasting and amicable relationship with the country's major selling agents. He also negotiated with the Inland Revenue Department for the standardisation of taxation for studmasters and breeders. And at a time when a scarcity of overseas funds hindered the industry's importation programme, Tom played a leading role in impressing on the Government of the time the need for reasonable facilities for the importation of stallions and female stock.

These challenges Tom managed with quiet diplomacy and dignity, always underpinned by his concern for the welfare of the small breeder.

RIGHT: Tom and Margot catch up on some sightseeing in Venice during their worldwide travels, which were often centred around racing.

Margot Lowry presented with a special posthumous certificate for Tom by Ron Trotter.
Also pictured from left: Peter Kelly, Patrick Hogan, Tommy Smith (in hat) and Joe Walls (right).

No-one could ever accuse Tom of flamboyancy, but his action in resolving a likely disaster at the 1966 national sales was spectacular. Australia had been hit by a currency crisis. Without hesitation and at short notice, Tom made a flying visit to Melbourne to speak to the Federal Treasurer in the hope of easing quota restrictions on Australian spending at Trentham. His efforts, to the relief of all concerned, were successful.

One of the association's most successful ventures under Tom's leadership was to change the attitude of the universities and their veterinary graduates toward horses. The association set up an equine branch to provide funds and scholarships, with some scholarships helping to send students overseas to complete projects pertaining to horses and the horse industry. This made a huge difference to the vets' interest in racing and to this day the scholarships continue.

As a result of his work with the Thoroughbred Breeders' Association, Tom also became very keen on the work of the Asian Racing Conference. The conference encompassed Japan, Hong Kong, Singapore, South Africa, Turkey, Australia and New Zealand. During the 1950s and 60s, Tom and Margot would travel to various venues, where there was a lot of flag-waving and entertainment. But importantly, good contacts were established and there was an increasing number of buyers for New Zealand's major yearling sales.

When it came to racing, Eddie Lowry always said he would be happy to pay 10 cents for every word Tom spoke, so wise and knowledgeable was the counsel. But Eddie said it was not only horse flesh or stock that he knew about. Tom knew every bloom in the garden; he knew about the flower of the kowhai tree and the timing of the pohutakawa tree's flowers; when the tuis would appear; the quality or otherwise of a piece of land. And his extensive travels gave him a sense of world events and their impact.

When Tom Junior moved to the Okawa homestead in 1976, there were still 20 broodmares of a high standard and, together with Captain Tim Rogers of Ireland, he imported Three Legs, who became New Zealand champion sire for three years. Tom Junior turned his stud into a thoroughly commercial grazing farm, looking after the mares for his family and other clients.

The annual draft of yearlings displayed at Okawa each New Year generally numbered between 15 and 20. During the 1980s, the yearling cheques were frequently more than $1 million. Through the 1990s, the Okawa Thoroughbred Horse Stud was still in the top 10 studs (stake winners to yearlings sold).

The family, carrying on the success of their father and grandfather, raced Hint, the South Island filly of the year and Cure, winner of the 1000 Guineas. Tom Junior, who won the Railway Group 1 with Lilt and the Thoroughbred Breeders' Stakes with Dare, bred or reared more than 25 stakes race winners.

SPRING 1976

NEW ZEALAND

Thoroughbred

75 cents   **BREEDERS' BULLETIN**

Tom Junior became what his grandfather had been, but never his father – president of the Hawke's Bay Jockey Club. Tom filled the vice-presidency for 14 years because Hylton Smith, president of the New Zealand Racing Conference, needed the Hawke's Bay position to continue the national role. Tom just got on with the committee work. Tom Junior's brother, Pat, was also heavily involved in racing in his home town of Taupo, developing the local picnic meeting into a club that at one point raced four times per year. Pat was president for 35 years.

While Tom and the rest of the family were in the racing game for business reasons, their sheer love of breeding, racing and winning was a motivating factor that drove them.

The certificate presented to Margot.

A budding owner once sought Tom's advice on the prospect of owning a group one horse. Tom, in his inimitable fashion, ruminated for a few moments and then replied: "Sit in front of an open fire for two years and each night throw a £100 note into the fire. At the end of two years think about whether you still want to do it."

Reflecting on the Lowry racing history, Tom Junior said: "Racing took four generations of Lowrys around the world to meet some great people and see some wonderful places. They would have been cash richer without the experience."

11. Life After Cricket

If racing became an all-consuming passion at the end of Tom's serious cricket phase, there was a multitude of other pursuits to occupy him in the aftermath of the 1937 comeback tour.

First, he made an unsuccessful foray into politics, with an attempt to win the National Party nomination for Rangitikei in 1938. This was two years after the formation of the National Party when three different factions – the Liberals, Democrats and Reform parties came together to try to curb the increasing popularity of the fresh and reforming social welfare Labour Government. Tom and the prospective National candidates were judged on how well their speeches went and how active they were and when it came to voting, those members had to try to overcome the interests of the disparate factions involved. Tom missed out, but this wasn't unusual for high-profile candidates in 1938. In Auckland Central, VC winner Reginald Judson suffered the same fate. On reflection, Tom may well have been thankful for not having made it to Parliament, despite his later success as a racing administrator and effective director on various boards. His man-of-the-land persona seemed ill-fitted to the hallowed halls of Parliament, although at that time, parliamentary duties were not the full-time occupation they are today.

Back at Moawhango, he continued to show his feel for the land. If the market was down he would buy "bones" and if the market was up he would buy "forward" cattle. (Bones refers to buying skinny cattle for fattening and then sending them off to market. It allows for quick turnover. Forward cattle had better breeding potential.)

He loved black cattle and if his man was in the corner of a paddock among a mob of 180 cattle, desperately trying to make a choice, Tom would exclaim: "The black one, the black one." The children learned more of this later when Tom, still drafting cattle on horseback late in life and with the kids on their ponies, would give them a hurry-up when they couldn't cut the right cattle. (Cutting the cattle is the art of isolating one from the mob.)

Again he would say "that one" and there would be a whole group of cattle. He always rode his much-loved big black horse, Ben, which most others were incapable of handling.

The horse riding became more than a work "vehicle" between 1937 and the war when he became an accomplished polo player for the Taihape club, playing in Savile Cup tournaments. Tom had a reputation for hitting the ball a long way and always said this was the best game of all to play.

While the Lowry tradition had been children's schooling with a governess on site, Margot decided a change of approach would be an advantage to her youngsters and enrolled them in the local school. The start date duly arrived and Margot loaded the children into a horse and trap to begin the journey. Within a short time the horse bolted and turned for home, a clear signal that the local school was out and the children would return to tuition with a governess,

President of the New Zealand Cricket Council. Attending a day's play against the MCC at Eden Park in 1951. From left: Tom, Giff Vivian, Dick Coates, unknown and England cricket captain Freddie Brown.

which occurred until they were a bit older.

Besides cricket, Tom pursued other outdoor activities, using his skill with a fishing rod to land trout out of the Tongariro River. Tom believed that the further you could cast the better the fish you would catch, so he bought a salmon rod and achieved his aim.

The duck-shooting season was also a time of regular excursions to one of his favourite mai-mais at Tokaanu, where regularly there would be bags of 300 ducks on opening day.

At the outbreak of war in 1939, Tom was 41 and tried to enlist for the army. Interviewed by the enlisting officer, he was asked: "How old are you?" Tom replied: "Thirty-four."

"Well, how come you were playing cricket for New Zealand when you were 16?" shot back the enlisting officer.

Age and the aftermath of a knee injury sustained from a polo pony fall discounted him being signed up and sampling the horrors of war.

In 1942, Tom's uncle, Eddie Watt, died, leaving him 80,000 acres of the Darr River Downs heritage property near Longreach in Queensland. Included in the bequest was also a large house in Sydney and Tom's advisers told him he should sell the property and keep the big house in Sydney. Darr River Downs was placed on the market at 7/6 an acre, but failed to find a buyer, so the house in Sydney was sold. When Darr River Downs was sold 50 years later for $3 million, the house value was more than $20 million, but as Tom Junior explained: "You have to eat and you can't get a feed out of a house."

Darr River Downs became a frequent visiting and working place for Tom and subsequently his sons. Eventually Tom had a manager on the property with half-shares. One day the manager approached Tom and said: "It's time one of us went." Tom, in typical fashion, fired back: "Okay, it's you."

Tom's father died in 1944, and Tom inherited Okawa. The days at Moawhango had at times been tough, especially during the depression years, but the over-riding memory of the family was of happy days. When he, Margot and the children arrived at Okawa, the thoroughbred stud became a huge focus, but it was still a mixed farm, and sheep and cattle were every bit as important as the horses. Tom used to say farming would be dreadfully boring if you didn't enjoy it, but what he enjoyed was the challenge of making it a successful business.

When the homestead needed repainting in the early 1950s, Heathcote Helmore, a prominent New Zealand architect, suggested to Margot it would be cheaper to build a new house rather than repaint the old. This appealed to Margot's creative senses and Faulkner Construction completed the one-and-a-half-storey house, limited because of building restrictions, at a cost of £25,000. The house, in all its splendour, still gazes down on the wonderful lawns and gardens and beyond to paddocks of grazing horses.

Margot was also involved in the building of the shepherds' cottage at Kiwirua (part of Okawa). A few years later, Tom called on one of the shepherds and pointed out there was a pig in the garden. The reply came back: "Gee boss, the missus will give it bloody hell when she comes home."

Taking account of the growing prestige of the stud, the stallion stables were also rebuilt in the early 1950s.

Being back at Okawa also gave Tom the chance to get the Grove cricket pitch prepared for more social Sunday matches. In most of these games he led his own private teams, or the Hastings club, against similar clubs, school teams or private sides such as the Eparaima Cricket Club. The ground had a concrete pitch, but the outfield was still rough, with the additional hazards of numerous clumps of thistles, and the sheep left-overs from recent grazing. The quality of the players varied.

Tom's brother-in-law, former England captain Percy Chapman, once hit three successive sixes there while scoring a century. A New Zealand captain Harry Cave, also scored a not out century there. Reg Bettington, with his leg-spinners, knew intimately how best to exploit the pitch intricacies. Others, because of age or lack of ability, were just social players, but Tom welcomed them all with a couple of provisos – they needed to give of their best in the field and the full rigour of the game had to be observed. This was an absolute must for Tom, who knew only one way to play the game, and that was tough but fair.

On one occasion, the visiting collegiate side was trying to win the match against the clock and a couple of over-excited scorers placed the wrong score on the board. When queried, the scorers insisted they were right. Shortly afterwards, according to the scoreboard, supported again by the scorers, the winning hit was made and stumps were drawn. Within a couple of minutes it was found that two runs were still needed, but by this time Tom and his henchman were removing the matting from the pitch and there was no chance of a resumption of play with Tom as captain.

Many young Hawke's Bay cricketers and promising schoolboy players turned out at Okawa. If they were observant and open to learning, all they needed was to watch "the Boss".

When an annual match against his old prep school, Hereworth, was rained out an hour or

LEFT: Still capable of holding his own at 60, Tom (right) marches out to bat with MCC secretary Ronnie Aird.

so before lunch, the headmaster suggested Tom give the boys a talk on cricket. "I don't suppose that I can tell the little so and sos anything much," said Tom. Then, to the astonishment of the older players present, he began on conventional lines by stressing the importance of first-rate gear and the correct turnout as the first requirement for a young cricketer. Tom himself was wearing dirty tennis shoes, black socks, aged white flannels and a grey pullover, while a nail was doing service for two fly buttons.

At Okawa once, his brother Jim, a good cricketer in his youth, was given out caught at the wicket and, disagreeing with the verdict, expressed his view forcibly to the umpire before leaving the field in high dudgeon. Near the boundary, he hurled his bat high into the air with an underarm swing. It lodged in a fork of a poplar and someone else had to retrieve it. "Jim always was a bloody fool," Tom observed philosophically.

The umpires were frequently under pressure. A batsman playing at a ball would hit the matting hard with his bat and that would produce a chorus of appeals from hopeful fieldsmen. The umpire would shake his head and Tom would remark: "It's amazing how many damn fools think it's out if you hit the matting with your bat."

A regular opponent was Stan Nowell-Usticke's side. That was, until another umpiring mishap. Stan had a reputation as a notoriously bad umpire and in the game in question was appealed to for a catch at the wicket. Unfortunately, Stan had been distracted by a chat with mid-on, and could give no decision. He consulted with the square leg umpire, who naturally couldn't see what had happened. Stan stalked back to his place, pondered for a moment, and then said: "Not-out." This was too much for Reg Bettington, who truculently asked: "Don't you know the laws of cricket?" Tom, in the role of peace-maker, endeavoured to dampen the fires of anger, but to no avail and Stan's team never returned to Okawa.

After Tom's side had been beaten by Wanganui Collegiate, someone suggested he strengthen Okawa by including some Hawke's Bay representatives. "Those useless buggers," Tom replied scathingly. "They never make a run."

He was equally scathing when Freddie Brown's 1951 touring MCC team blamed their lack of aggression and strokeplay on the slowness of the New Zealand pitches. Tom responded: "I never knew a pitch yet on which you couldn't drive a half volley for four."

His appreciation of aggressive play and objection to too much New Zealand prodding and leaving of the ball was equally shown in a remark he made to a visiting player at Maowhango. The batsman punched the first ball for four, and anticipated a short one next from the bowler. He was ready for the bouncer and hooked it far over the square leg boundary. "It's obvious you learnt your cricket outside this country," muttered Tom to the Australian.

Remarkably, Tom showed no inclination to give up the game. One time the Wanganui Collegiate school team was collapsing against Reg Bettington's bowling. Tom then bowled an over to RM Young, the only batsman offering resistance, and considering he was 54 he bowled it extremely well. Unfortunately for his plans, the batsman took a single off the fifth ball. At the end of the over an older member of his side called out: "Well bowled Tom."

"Well bowled! What bloody use was that over? I've merely got the wrong man down at Reg's end," replied Tom.

In another match against Wanganui Collegiate at Okawa, Tom was late arriving, so David Orton tossed in his place with the opposing skipper, Dick Sewell. When Tom arrived,

Tom and his brother-in-law, Percy Chapman, enjoy a game of golf during one of Percy's visits to New Zealand.

Still interested in the property in his twilight years.

Orton told his skipper that he had lost the toss and they were in the field. After telling Orton he had no authority, he immediately summonsed Sewell and said there was to be a re-toss. Tom proceeded to win the toss and then batted most of the day.

When Tom was about 60 and Harry Cave not much beyond his prime as one of New

Zealand's best bowlers, there was a great duel on the Collegiate ground, with the pitch helpful to seamers. Neither of the former test captains was prepared to give an inch. Tom vigilantly crouched over his bat and Harry put all he had into each delivery. At last Tom saw off the bowler, only to relax concentration and follow a gentle in-swinger from Dick Sewell straight into short leg's hands.

After matches at the Grove, the participants would retreat to the Okawa homestead, where Margot would dispense lavish hospitality. The young men would drink beer and the oldies whisky. Some of the teams would stay at the Hawke's Bay Club, where the boys would be sent out in the morning to find milk to add to the whisky. These after-match affairs could extend long after the game. One such after-match gathering gradually thinned out well after it became dark, leaving only a hard core of men to rake over the day's events and the battles of earlier years. It was said the party broke up only because Tom ran out of matches to light his cigarettes.

Through his post-cricket years, Tom's health was generally good and at 50 he could still lift a wool bale on his own. But he frequently had a bad back (probably from lifting hay bales) and would periodically suffer from lumbago and need to go to bed for a while. He was also subject to gout, no doubt as a result of his frequent imbibing. He graduated from whisky to a liking for gin and soda or gin and water. It was the days before breathalysers. When they were introduced, he said: "It won't make a difference to me because if I don't have a drink for the rest of my life I'll always get a positive."

His drinking never seemed to impair his judgement. Tom Junior used to take Tom and his brother Jim to jockey club meetings and annual meetings, where the club would shout for members, and it would turn into a hectic night. Tom Junior remembers his father saying to him: "I think Uncle Jimmy might have had one or two. We'll wait until he's had a couple more, then you might like to take him down to the car." So Tom Junior took his godfather to the car to the accompaniment of Jimmy's customary "dear boy, dear boy". Back at the gathering, Tom Junior told his father Jim was safely in the car, whereupon Tom said: "We'll just have another one or two." When eventually they arrived at the car, Uncle Jimmy had returned to the function. As Tom Junior explained: "They both enjoyed a noggin."

Smoking may have been a bigger problem. Tom became a virtual chain-smoker, lighting a new one from that just completed. The smoking addiction had resulted from the free cigarettes handed out during the time of his pilot training in World War I. Margot smoked as well. Son Pat described how Margot used to do the cooking while smoking a cigarette, with the ash going into the soup or the scrambled eggs. After dinner they would all sit at the table and Margot would say: "Tom, what about a cigarette?" and he would throw them down, followed by the matches and she would have to catch them. Pat said they both smoked with the windows up in the car, a crucial reason for him never taking up the habit.

Tom's Grove cricket may have been recreational, a welcome relief from the hard slog of the farm and the horse stud, but that was only part of it. His racing administration could be time-consuming. He also sat on various boards, including Barraud and Abraham, the seed merchants, when he lived in Taihape, and later Williams and Kettle and, for a long period, the Napier Harbour Board, which he enjoyed.

During his Williams and Kettle directorship, the firm was having a hard time in tough

Tom gave Kel Tremain a helping hand during his All Black career.

economic conditions, when a rugby player of exceptional qualities, Kel Tremain, joined the firm. In 1963 Tremain was selected for the All Blacks tour of the United Kingdom and the general manager announced to his board that "we can't afford to give him the time off". Tom didn't hesitate, telling him: "Either send him on tour or you'll lose me." Kel Tremain was grateful for that.

His association with cricket at the top level was less frequent, although he became the New Zealand Cricket Council president in 1950, taking over from Arthur Donnelly, and serving until 1953. Periodically he was called on by the media to comment on aspects of the game. When John Reid's team was about to tour England in 1958, he was interviewed by the old New Zealand Broadcasting Service and, using his knowledge of English conditions, made some pertinent points about what Reid and his team would need to do to achieve success. In the interview, Tom sounds considered and articulate, displaying a deep baritone voice with rounded, cultured vowels. The archived interview is notable for retaining a decent smoker's cough right at the end, surprisingly not edited out.

Tom was never one to decry modern players at the expense of their predecessors. In an interview in the *New Zealand Herald* in the early 1960s, he considered the overall standard superior to his day, but he was quick to point out the quality of his special players – Stewie Dempster, Roger Blunt and Giff Vivian – who, he said, would have succeeded in any era. While Dennis Silk's MCC team was touring New Zealand in 1962-63, he made a plea in London papers for faster, truer wickets, claiming that in his day the wickets were better and scores of 400 runs in an innings were not unusual.

The family held great importance for him, although it was Margot who kept the extended

Checking the form. Another day at the races with Margot.

family ties alive and well. There were always lots of family and relations, as well as friends and acquaintances, to stay and Tom was very welcoming to his guests.

Beet Chapman would always turn up after golf on Sunday, brother Jim and his wife, Edna, were frequent visitors, and so were the Bettingtons. These visits would often extend to family tennis matches, when there was some intense friendly rivalry. Tom, Jim and Reg could

Tom leading Carol on Tile at Okawa, 1945.

place the ball anywhere on court and would have their opponents running from side to side. None of them would tolerate double faults.

Surprisingly, Tom gave no cricket instruction or coaching to Tom Junior or Pat. It was as if Tom felt he shouldn't impose an expectation on the boys to succeed in something he had been good at. Tom Junior said later that he never knew his father was a prominent New Zealand cricketer until someone outside the family told him when he was 13. Pat said they were encouraged by Margot to try plenty of things and then concentrate on what they liked the most. The boys, unquestionably, were somewhat in awe of their father as youngsters, but once they hit their teenage years and worked with him on the land, they became much closer. They would accompany him to Darr River Downs in Queensland, or for special trips to Australia to see some cricket.

The youngest in the family, Carol, spent more time with him while growing up owing to Ann and the boys being older and off doing their own things. "I would go around the sheep with dad, but would be sent out of sight if a ewe had to be helped to lamb. He didn't think that sheep yards were a good place for girls, either. Too much swearing probably. And he didn't like us going near stables when the stallions were busy. Also, I went with him and the stock agent to pick cattle. I had to be the dog on the horse trying to draft the chosen ones from the mob, which was good fun. And we all did a stint in the stables helping prepare yearlings for annual sales."

Tom acquired the sobriquet "the Boss" from Margot and it spread far and wide, although he would often call Margot "the Boss" as well. There was no question he could be strict. The children were required to change for dinner and put on shoes. Carol recently attended a school reunion where a friend reminded her how her father had told her firmly that she must wear shoes to the dinner table. But once at the dinner table he had no inclination to dominate the conversation. He would listen to everyone talking, discussing and arguing, and sum up with a one-liner which was frequently hilarious. He never wasted words or pontificated.

Around the dining room table, the family would play fascinating card games. Tom would participate in a game called Racing Demons, playing with two hands, to the protests of his children, who said it wasn't allowed. The only exception to the dining table formality was on a Friday night, when their meal (usually fish) could be eaten in the kitchen.

Tom loved a picnic, but done with simplicity. A loaf of white bread, a can of sardines or tinned tongues, asparagus. Cut a thick doorstep of bread and put on heaps of butter and the fillings. Normally he liked nothing better than cold meat and pickled onions, but he hated anything oiled or with garlic. When it came to fish, he would head the Super Snipe in the direction of the Dominion Fish Shop in Hastings, one of his favourites. While he never gardened himself, after being out on the land he would arrive at the house with a bunch of violets or raspberries placed on a big rhubarb leaf.

One thing that Tom could never be accused of was sartorial elegance. On the farm he would usually be dressed in an old pair of grey trousers (with cuffs for the cigarette ash) and shirt and black jersey, very worn at the elbows, and a battered old felt hat (when he was getting into the car he didn't like the hat to be knocked off his head). On one occasion, someone arrived at the door and asked him if Mr Lowry was about. Tom said: "Yes, hello." Most would have said he had poor dress sense. But on the other hand his breeding never allowed him to drop his standards for special occasions, and with his powerful figure he could cut a fine presence wearing a formal suit at the races or a dinner of note. His 1937 team members in England never forgot his sartorial appearance for the King's coronation.

Conversely, Tom liked the women in the family to look good and they did. But he always had great concern for their welfare. He liked listening to them talk rather than leading the conversation, although he and Margot engaged in frequent discussions about racing.

For entertainment, he enjoyed all the musicals and especially the classical works of Beethoven. The wireless was an essential adjunct to his racing and cricket interests and he would stay glued to its vicinity, particularly at the weekends. When television arrived, he became a confirmed Western watcher. Carol also remembers going to the cinema with him after he had expressed an interest in seeing what Elizabeth Taylor really looked like. After buying Jaffas, Tom promptly fell asleep, only to be suddenly awoken by the sound of Jaffas rolling down the slope on the wooden floor. Tom's startled wake-up response was, "Where is she?" just as she was arriving on the boat.

Periodically Sunday church would be held at the local Pukehamoamoa School, and this was the scene of more humour as Carol and Margot watched Tom squeeze into a small primary school desk while listening to an esoteric sermon from the arch-deacon. This was all taken in good part because of his desire not to cause a fuss, just as he would display manners of a bygone era. When a new local minister first visited Tom at Okawa, he was taken by Tom to all the houses on the estate and introduced to the people. This, for Tom, was right and proper and the courteous thing to do.

Tom's generosity was legendary, although he objected to being pestered for annual subscriptions, usually telling such canvassers he wasn't interested in paying a few dollars a year as he was bound to forget to pay his dues. "Come to me if you get stuck for money," he would say and they knew £50 or £100 would be on the way if they asked.

When a colts cricket tour was under discussion, the question of expenses would be high on the agenda. "I suppose some of us will have to put our hands in our pockets," observed Tom, which meant he would foot the bill himself. While born into privilege, the depression had curbed any unnecessary wastage, but occasionally he would splash out. At one stage the banks changed the way they presented their statements. Tom knew he was running an overdraft and was surprised to see the figures were all in black, without detecting "DR" beside the final number. Tom immediately rang his broker and bought 20,000 Wattie's shares. They soon went up by two shillings and he had no trouble paying back the money he had spent.

Through all this, Tom remained an uncomplicated, straightforward man, totally without pretension. He could present a somewhat stern countenance, but over-riding this slightly irascible exterior was his personal charm and innate kindness. Locals beat a steady path to his door, treating him like a counsellor and mentor. They ranged from racing people to local Maori. He had mana and they liked him. One of the last times an old friend, HEB Newton, saw him was when he reached the Grove at Okawa an hour before the start of play, when no other players or spectators had arrived, to see a lonely figure in an old felt hat laboriously pushing a marker round the boundary.

This by a man about whom the following remark was once made at a dinner party by his racing friend Alan Marshall. At the dinner table Marshall conspiratorially leaned forward and said in hushed tones: "Did you hear about poor old Tom Lowry?" The conversation immediately ceased and the guests moved in to hear the worst. "The poor old fellow has just come into another million."

Tom was certainly something of a legend for his wealth, but no person displayed it less ostentatiously. He seldom spoke about money and never, ever talked about his achievements.

No-one is able to explain why he never received a King's or Queen's honour. The pioneering aspects of many of his achievements seemed ample qualification for a knighthood or other top award, based on most recent examples. By the time his cricket feats had ended a Labour Government was in power for an extended period and this may have been a factor. His undoubted wealth would certainly not have helped him gain sympathy from that quarter.

His last head groom, Eddie Lowry, may have been the only person he ever discussed the matter with and Eddie was left with the lasting impression that if an honour had been offered he would never have accepted.

In June 1976, he made his last public appearance, at the Filly of the Year dinner, and failed to complete his acceptance speech for Mop's award. He was clearly not his old self. Three weeks later Tom Junior was taking him around the property and stopped the vehicle to open a gate. As he got out, Tom, sitting in the passenger's seat, had a stroke that killed him. There were two lighted cigarettes in the car ashtray, one just completed and one ready to go. He was 78.

LEFT: The cigarette still burning, but life slowly fading.

There were 800 at the funeral at St Matthew's Church in Hastings, where the Vicar of Puketapu said: "The fair-mindedness, chivalry and strong character which he displayed on the cricket field were exemplified in his business dealings and in the world of horse-racing." The tributes came from many quarters. George Donnelly, president of the Hawke's Bay Jockey Club, said: "He was a real man in all ways with an unforgettable personality and charm." Donnelly added: "He was the elder statesman of racing and breeding in Hawke's Bay and, to an extent, the whole country."

The president of the Thoroughbred Breeders' Association said: "We can look back with pride when we say, 'I knew Tom Lowry'."

From the cricket world, leading writer Dick Brittenden wrote: "This remarkable man has left an indelible mark on New Zealand cricket...is perhaps the most colourful character in the whole history of New Zealand cricket."

In the English *Cricketer*, Alex Wilkinson said: "At times Tom may have assumed the attitude of 'tough guy', but he had a heart of gold and many benefited from his generosity."

Finally, in a newspaper obituary, Tom's family remembered him as "a quiet and kindly man who disliked fuss and ostentation".

Epilogue

Whenever the history of New Zealand cricket and racing is discussed, Tom Lowry's name resurfaces. While many of his contemporaries have faded in the public consciousness, Tom retains a lustre that reflects his great contribution and larger-than-life personality.

In the year of Tom's death Don Neely, in the *DB Cricket Annual*, interviewed Jack Phillipps, much-respected former New Zealand (and MCC) touring manager, and asked him if he were to tour England again, which 16 players he would pick from the 30-odd years he was intimately involved at the top level.

Phillipps rather complicated things for himself by including five captains – Tom Lowry, John Reid, Walter Hadlee, Geoff Rabone and Merv Wallace. Neely then asked: "Who would you entrust with the captaincy and why?" Phillipps was unhesitating: "Tom Lowry would certainly be my first choice. He was designed by nature. I once heard him described as a man more given to command than obey. If you put 11 players through a gate on to a cricket field and Tom Lowry was one of them, I think most people would say, 'Well, there's the skipper'. He had that sort of air of command about him. He was an innovator. I don't think Tom ever took a fixed plan on to the field and I don't think a good captain should. Cricket is not a predictable game, but Tom always had a counter for the batsman's moves and when he was batting I think that the bowlers felt he accounted for their moves too."

Sportspeople (as in other walks of life) can only meet the challenge of their own time and as history marches on just a handful can expect to be plucked from the past to be placed with any surety in "all-time great" player or team lists. As a batsman Tom certainly met the challenge of his time, but his record would have not be sufficient to make a dream New Zealand X1. Name a handful of outstanding captains, though, and Tom is definitely among the best.

Jack Phillipps' choice of Tom as the best touring captain, it could be argued, would have extended to the leader for all matches, in the time between our first official test and the year of the Tom's death. Beyond that, other skippers come into the reckoning. Stephen Fleming, as the most successful, and Geoff Howarth, close behind, would be candidates with indisputable qualifications. Martin Crowe is another. Where Tom stands out is with the sheer force of personality and command and probably only John Reid matches him in this respect.

Like Tom, Reid, too, had sometimes to lead teams of dubious quality against much better opponents and because of this, the need to show the way in every aspect of the game was the driving force behind their methods. What Tom added in abundance was innovation and restless, constant change to unsettle superior opposition.

Given a modern-day team to lead, Tom would not have tolerated too much player power. He was a dominant leader not given over to unnecessary interference with his plans. This put him more in the category of an Ian Chappell, but like Chappell he would have encouraged team cohesion with dressing-room camaraderie. Whether he could have achieved it over a glass of beer and a cigarette is another question.

He was never overly tested by the media (in the age before constant television exposure), but once he got over an early suspicion he knew how to deal with the cricket correspondents (and later racing writers), employing a combination of "matter of fact" and personal charm. In later life, when his son, Tom Junior, became prominent in racing circles, Tom encouraged him to cultivate and treat the media with respect.

Like John Reid, Tom would have relished playing limited-overs cricket. Everything in his make-up was designed to take the game by the scruff of the neck, and with his all-round skills he would have been involved at every turn. His frequent bowling changes would not have been so noticeable and would have been seen more as just part of the game.

Eighty years after leading New Zealand in their first official test, Tom remains at or near the top of our best. As Raymond Robertson-Glasgow so aptly described, he was "a leader in a thousand".

After his death, Tom's contribution was honoured in a variety of ways. The New Zealand Sports Hall of Fame, founded in 1990 to honour 150 years of organised settlement, has now honoured just 13 cricketers. Glenn Turner, Bert Sutcliffe, John Reid, Stewie Dempster and Martin Donnelly were inaugural inductees. Richard Hadlee and Walter Hadlee followed in 1993 and 1995 respectively, and then in 1996 Tom and Jack Cowie were inducted. Others added since have been Dick Motz, Dan Reese, Ian Smith and Martin Crowe.

The New Zealand Thoroughbred Breeders' Association made a special posthumous presentation, accepted by Margot, honouring his service to the thoroughbred industry.

Tom and Jack Cowie were inducted into the New Zealand Sports Hall of Fame at a function at Eden Park in 1996. Back row: Tom Lowry Junior, Terry Jarvis, Paddianne and Don Neely, Norma and Bert Sutcliffe. Front row: Eric Tindill, his daughter Molly and Jack Cowie's daughters, Janet Roberts and Sue Taylor.

Among the dignitaries who attended were Patrick Hogan, Sydney trainer Tommy Smith, commentator Peter Kelly and auctioneer Joe Walls, while the presentation was made by Ron Trotter. And as recently as 2008, the Lowry name was still making headlines when Desert Gold was inducted into the Racing Hall of Fame.

When it came to writing Tom's biography, all but a couple of his cricket contemporaries had died. Eric Tindill was still alive, at 99 the oldest living test cricketer, but unfortunately he was no longer capable of relating past memories.

Tom Pritchard, New Zealand representative, occasional team-mate of Tom and Warwickshire fast bowler, was 92 when I interviewed him and he revelled in the deeds of Tom who he thought was a "cracking" bloke. "It's so very nice that you are writing about him because it's nice to write about nice people."

Like Tom's sisters, Beet and Marion, his brothers, Jim and Ralph, were colourful characters. Jim farmed Oreka, a part of Okawa where the hot dry hillsides were exposed to the westerly winds. Because of this, the land was often short of green grass. This made his farming more difficult and left him, as he described it, short of "boodle" (money). After getting his tennis Blue at Cambridge, he continued to play many tournaments around New Zealand. Towards the end of his tennis days, when the opposition was getting on top of him, he would call his cairn terriers, wicked little dogs with adorable faces, on to the court. By the time the umpire had cleared the court the opponent was so frustrated that JN, as he was affectionately known, had regained the initiative. A family favourite, Jim died without an enemy.

Ralph, on the other hand, may have upset a few acquaintances along the way, including his own children. He was a brilliant, visionary farmer and not afraid to take on debt to buy more land. Ralph had won his rugby Blue at Cambridge and later represented Wanganui-King Country against the 1930 British Lions. Described as the maverick of the family, he was good looking, a ladies' man and married three times. His son, Peter, described him as a man driven by what he wanted to do. Among his diverse talents was the authoring of a book called *Taihape, Live Happy Die Happy*, which seems to have summed up Ralph's philosophy on life. Peter said he and his siblings and mother were fortunate in the way Tom and Margot and Reg and Marion Bettington gave them such a continuing sense of family after Ralph had departed for his second marriage.

When Tom died, Margot commissioned Peter McIntyre to paint a portrait of him, hoping that more than in a photograph, he would be able to capture the real Tom, "who was so full of warmth, kindness and humour". The portrait today hangs in the upper hallway at Okawa. Pat also has a Peter McIntyre painting (reproduced on the front cover), of the Grove cricket ground, hanging at his property in Taupo.

Margot Lowry lived for a further 17 years after Tom's death, continuing her work with the Red Cross and Plunket and maintaining her contact with her family and friends of all ages. Pat said Margot had a way of building people up when they were down and taking away the ladder from those who had climbed too high.

Tom and Margot's oldest child, Ann, married Peter Pinkney. At their wedding reception in the garden at Okawa, with everyone invited, one of the aunts told another that it was the "Third Battle of Hastings". In answer to the question, "What was the second?", she said: "Your wedding, dearie."

Just six years after Tom's death, Ann and Peter died tragically when a Bell Ranger helicopter they were in crashed near Riversdale in Southland. They were part-owners of the largest privately-owned sheep station in New Zealand – Glenaray Station at Waikaia.

All three of Ann's siblings continue to run fulfilling, active lives.

Tom Junior, who inherited Okawa from Tom, married Jane de Gruchy. Jane, like her predecessors at Okawa, was influential in enhancing the buildings and gardens. Tom Junior, as detailed in the racing chapter, continued many of his father's activities. After Jane died, he remarried to racing driver Angus Hyslop's delightful widow, Joanna, and together they continue to bring a sense of joie de vivre to life at the Okawa homestead.

Pat married a Wellingtonian, Jane Hewitt, and the couple have spent their married life farming at Taupo. Pat played second X1 cricket at school, had a great eye and was in the school shooting team, and later became master of the Taupo Hunt. Pat believed he inherited the Russell legs, well suited to the military, but not necessarily for sports like cricket.

Carol certainly made the family sit up and take notice when she married Frenchman, Phillipe Marie. Tom's reaction was: "What's wrong with a good New Zealand farmer?" and he could probably foresee difficulties arising. They did and the marriage ended. Carol is a capable masters skier, and from her home base in Christchurch she still, in her mid-60s, skis regularly. Like the rest of the family, she follows thoroughbred racing, and she owns two broodmares, as well as pursuing her hobbies of languages, music and gardening.

Five generations (with Tommy now leasing the land from his father) have maintained Okawa as a productive and economical unit, working with the ebb and flow of nature and dealing with the peaks and troughs of economic life. No-one can predict whether 160-odd years of Lowry residency will turn into a double-century, but whatever the future holds, the Lowrys have undoubtedly done much for the well-being and betterment of New Zealand.

Statistical Record

THOMAS COLEMAN LOWRY

BORN:	February 17, 1898, Fernhill, Hawke's Bay.
DIED:	July 20, 1976, Okawa, Hastings.
MAJOR TEAMS:	New Zealand, Auckland, Cambridge University, Somerset, MCC, Wellington.
BATTING STYLE:	Right-hand bat.
FIELDING POSITION:	Part-time wicketkeeper.

BATTING AND FIELDING

	M	I	NO	RUNS	HS	AVE	100	50	CT	ST
Tests	7	8	0	223	80	27.87	0	2	8	0
First-class	198	322	20	9421	181	31.19	18	47	188	49

BOWLING

	M	BALLS	RUNS	WKTS	BB	AVE	ECON	SR	4W
Tests	7	12	5	0	-	-	2.50	-	0
First-class	198	2887	1323	49	4/14	27.00	2.74	58.9	0

FIRST-CLASS CRICKET *Season by season*

BATTING

	M	I	NO	RUNS	HS	AVE	100	50	CT	ST
1917-18 NZ	2	4	0	48	28	12.00	0	0	2	1
1919 England	1	2	0	0	0	0.00	0	0	2	0
1921 England	13	25	0	648	81	25.92	0	5	9	0
1922 England	18	30	2	666	77	23.78	0	3	20	8
1922-23 Australia	5	8	0	118	45	14.75	0	0	3	1
1922-23 NZ	8	11	0	355	130	32.27	1	2	6	1
1923 England	25	47	3	1564	161	35.54	4	8	36	2
1924 England	22	35	2	868	133	26.30	1	6	17	7
1925-26 Australia	4	7	0	213	123	30.42	1	0	4	3
1926-27 NZ	3	6	0	296	110	49.33	1	1	0	0
1927 England	25	37	4	1277	106	38.69	4	6	20	5
1927-28 Australia	1	2	0	79	44	39.50	0	0	0	3
1927-28 NZ	8	13	1	563	181	46.91	1	3	12	0

1928-29 NZ	3	5	0	251	134	50.20	1	0	1	0
1929-30 NZ	8	12	0	402	122	33.50	1	2	12	0
1930-31 NZ	3	6	0	272	91	45.33	0	3	2	0
1931 England	30	43	3	1286	129	32.15	2	8	29	5
1931 Scotland	1	1	0	4	4	4.00	0	0	0	1
1931-32 NZ	3	4	1	53	43	17.66	0	0	2	0
1932-33 NZ	2	4	0	41	19	10.25	0	0	1	0
1937 England	10	14	2	346	121	28.83	1	0	6	12
1937 Scotland	1	2	0	27	18	13.50	0	0	1	0
1937 Ireland	1	2	1	36	30no	36.00	0	0	1	0
1937-38 Australia	1	2	1	8	8no	8.00	0	0	2	0

BOWLING

	BALLS	MDNS	RUNS	WKTS	BB	AVE
1919 England	36	2	20	1	1-20	20.00
1921 England	114	1	84	2	1-16	42.00
1923 England	54	1	34	1	1-22	34.00
1924 England	12	0	5	0		
1927 England	1040	30	450	15	3-13	30.00
1927-28 NZ	425	6	231	11	3-27	21.00
1928-29 NZ	318	16	102	3	1-12	34.00
1929-30 NZ	228	14	105	1	1-64	105.00
1931 England	618	26	274	15	4-14	18.26
1931-32 NZ	42	2	18	0		

ARTHUR PERCY FRANK CHAPMAN

BORN: September 3, 1900, The Mount, Reading, Berkshire.
DIED: September 16, 1961, Alton, Hampshire.
MAJOR TEAMS: England, Cambridge University, MCC, Kent.
BATTING STYLE: Left-hand bat.

BATTING AND FIELDING

	M	I	NO	RUNS	HS	AVE	100	50	6S	CT	ST
Tests (1924-31)	26	36	4	925	121	28.90	1	5	12	32	0
First-class (1920-39)	394	554	44	16309	260	31.97	27	75	356	0	0

BOWLING

	M	BALLS	RUNS	WKTS	BBM	AVE
Tests	26	40	20	0	-	-
First-class	394	1576	921	22	5/40	41.86

REGINALD HENSHALL BRINDLEY BETTINGTON

BORN:	February 24, 1900, Oatlands, Parramatta, New South Wales, Australia.
DIED:	June 24, 1969, Gisborne, New Zealand.
MAJOR TEAMS:	Oxford University, Middlesex, MCC, New South Wales.
BATTING STYLE:	Right-hand bat.
BOWLING:	Leg-break and googly.

BATTING AND FIELDING

	M	I	NO	RUNS	HS	AVE	100	50	CT
First-class (1920-38)	86	142	21	3314	127	27.38	4	8	60

BOWLING

BALLS	MDNS	RUNS	WKTS	BB	AVE	5WI
14788	368	8496	357	8-66	23.79	21

Bibliography

Altham, HS. *A History of Cricket Vol 1*. George Allen & Unwin, 1962.

Appleby, Mathew. *New Zealand Test Cricket Captains*. Reed Publishing NZ Ltd, 2002.

Auckland Cricket Association. *100 Not Out, A Centennial History of the Auckland Cricket Association*. 1983.

Batty, Mike. *Bill Bernau and the New Zealand Cricket Tour of England 1927*. Wordself Press, 2001.

Brew, Steve. *Greycliffe: Stolen Lives*. Navarine Publishing, 2003.

Brittenden RT. *Big Names in New Zealand Cricket*. Moa Publications Ltd, 1983.

Brittenden RT. *A Century of Cricket, The History of the Canterbury Cricket Association 1877-1977*. Canterbury Cricket Association, 1977.

Brittenden, RT. *Great Days in New Zealand Cricket*. A.H. & A.W. Reed, 1958.

Cane FF. *Cricket Centenary, The Story of Cricket in Hawke's Bay 1855-1955*. FF Cane Publications, 1959.

Canynge Caple, C. *The All Blacks at Cricket*. Littlebury & Co Ltd, 1958.

Canynge Caple, S. *England versus New Zealand 1902-1949*. Barcliff Advertising & Publishing Co. Ltd, 1949.

Carman, Arthur H. *New Zealand International Cricket 1894-1974*. Sporting Publications, 1975.

Chesterton George and Doggart Hubert. *Oxford and Cambridge Cricket*. Willow Books Collins, 1989.

Coldham, James D. *Lord Harris*. George Allen & Unwin, 1983.

Costello, John and Finnegan, Pat. *Tapestry of Turf, The History of New Zealand Racing*. Moa Publications Ltd, 1988.

Costello, John. *New Zealand Galloping Greats*. Moa Publications, 1977.

Cotter, Gerry. *England versus New Zealand*. Crowood Press, 1990.

Croudy, Brian (The Association of Cricket Statisticians). *A Guide to First Class Matches Played in New Zealand 1863-1980*. 1981.

Crowley, Brian. *History of Australian Bowling*. McMillan Co, 1986.

Douglas, Christopher. *Douglas Jardine – Spartan Cricketer*. George Allen & Unwin, 1995.

Down, Michael. *Archie – A Biography of Archie MacLaren*. George Allen & Unwin Ltd, 1981.

Ferguson, WH. *Mr Cricket*. Nicholas Kaye Ltd, 1960.

Fidian, Marc. *Australian Cricket – Doctors & Dentists*. Pakenham Gazette, 1993.

Foot, David. *Cricket's Unholy Trinity*. Stanley Paul, 1995.

Frindall, Bill. *The Wisden Book of Test Cricket 1876/77 to 1977/78*. McDonald & James, 1979.

Frith, David. *The Archie Jackson Story.* The Cricketer, 1974.

Hadlee, Walter. *The Innings of a Lifetime.* David Bateman, 1993.

Hedley, Alex. *Fernleaf Cairo.* Harper Collins, 2009.

Hintz OS. *The New Zealanders in England 1931.* J.M. Dent & Sons Ltd, 1931.

Hopkins, Jim (editor). *Words on Wings – An Anthology of New Zealanders of Flight.* H Collins NZ Ltd, 2004.

King, Michael. *The Penguin History of New Zealand.* Penguin, 2003.

Kynaston, David. *Archie's Last Stand – MCC in New Zealand 1922-23.* Queen Anne Press, 1984.

Lemmon, David. *Percy Chapman – A Biography.* Queen Anne Press, 1985.

Lowry, Ralph. *Taihape, Be Happy Die Happy.* Private Publication, c1982.

Malies, Jeremy. *Sporting Doubles.* Robson Books Ltd, 1998.

McConnell Lynn, Smith Ian. *The New Zealand Shell Cricket Encyclopaedia.* Moa Beckett, 1993.

McLean, TP. *Silver Fern – 150 years of New Zealand Sport.* Moa Publications, 1990.

McMillan, Neville. *New Zealand Sporting Legends.* Moa Beckett, 1983.

Neely DO, King RP, Payne FK. *Men in White.* Moa Publications, 1986.

Neely, Don. *100 Summers.* Moa Publishing, 1975.

Nye, Rod. *Martin Donnelly.* Harper Collins, 1999.

Paice, Edward. *Lost Lion of Empire.* Harper Collins, 2002.

Pollard, Jack. *Six and Out, The Legend of Australia and New Zealand Cricket.* A.H. & A.W. Reed, 1970.

Prittie, Terence. *Middlesex County Cricket Club.* Convoy Publications, 1951.

Reese TW. *N.Z. Cricket 1841-1914.* Simpson and Williams, 1927.

Reese TW. *N.Z. Cricket 1914-1933.* Whitcombe & Tombs Ltd, 1936.

Reese, Dan. *Was it All Cricket?* George Allen & Unwin Ltd, 1948.

Rickard LS. *Three Schools, A Centennial History.* Hereworth School Trust, 1989.

Robertson-Glasgow, RC. *Cricket Prints.* T. Werner Laurie Ltd, 1948.

Robertson-Glasgow, RC. *46 Not Out.* Hollis and Carter, 1948.

Robinson, Tony (editor). *West to the Annie.* RD9 Historical Committee, Reprint 2003.

Roebuck, Peter. *From Sammy to Jimmy, The Official History of the Somerset County Cricket Club.* Partridge Press, 1991.

Romanos, Joseph. *Merv Wallace – A Cricket Master.* Joel Publishing, 2000.

Smith, Nigel. *Kiwis Declare.* Random House, 1994.

Swanton, EW. *As I Said at the Time.* Unwin Paperbacks, 1986.

Swanton, EW. *Gubby Allen – Man of Cricket.* Hutchinson/Stanley Paul & Co Ltd, 1985.

Todd, Sydney. *Sporting Records of New Zealand.* Moa Publications, 1976.

Turnbull MJ and Allom MJC. *The Book of The Two Maurices.* E Allom & Co. Ltd, 1930.

Waugh, Evelyn. *Brideshead Revisited.* Little, Brown & Co, United States paperback, 1999.

Wynne-Thomas, Peter. *The Complete History of Cricket Tours.* Hamlyn Publishing Group Ltd, 1989.

ANNUALS AND ALMANACKS

Wisden – various.

New Zealand Cricket Almanack – various.

DB Cricket Annual – various.

New Zealand Cricket Council annual reports 1911-1953.

Christ's College Register – various.

The Cricketer magazine.

New Zealand Cricket magazine.

New Zealand Thoroughbred Breeders' Bulletin.

PAPERS

Lowry, Peter. *The Lowry Family in NZ.* Family Tree, 2002.

RML-S. *Early Tales of the Lowry Family 1846-1897.* 1947.

HEB Newton. *A tribute to T.C. Lowry.* c1961.

SCRAPBOOKS

1927 tour – Pat Lowry.

1931 tour (two versions) – Graham Vivian.

1937 tour – Graham Vivian.

AUDIO

Sound Archives Nga Taonga Korero – Tom Lowry interview. 1958.

Winston McCarthy on 1931 tour. c1950.

Index

About the Author

Bill Francis is well-known as a long-standing radio leader, most notably as the manager of the hugely-successful Newstalk ZB brand, as well as Radio Sport. His early broadcasting days were spent as a sports journalist, commentator and editor, and for many years he commentated on cricket in Waikato, Otago and Auckland. His passion for cricket has continued as a director of Auckland Cricket and, more recently, as a board member of New Zealand Cricket. Bill lives in Auckland with his wife Mary. He has three married children and four grandsons. His previous books were:

Promote Your Sport, 1993

And Then There Were Ten, The Francis's of Masterton, 1997

Inside Talk Radio, 2002

ZB, The Voice of an Iconic Radio Station, 2006

Tom Lowry is his fifth book.